ERIC

LOUIS

KOHLER

IN THE

ACCOUNTING

PROFESSION

NANCY A. WAGNER

ERIC LOUIS KOHLER IN THE ACCOUNTING PROFESSION

by
Nancy A. Wagner
Department of Accounting
Georgia Southern College

Research Monograph No. 100

1987

Business Publishing Division
College of Business Administration
Georgia State University
Atlanta, Georgia

Library of Congress Cataloging in Publication Data

Wagner, Nancy A.
  Eric Louis Kohler in the accounting profession.

  (Research monograph ; no. 100)
  Includes bibliographies.
1. Kohler, Eric Louis, 1892-1976. 2. Accountants—United States. 3. Accounting—United States. I. Title. II. Ser:
Research monograph (Georgia State University. College of Business Administration) ; no. 100.

HF5604.5.K64W34   1987   657'.092'4   86-25633
ISBN 0-88406-196-5

Business Publishing Division
College of Business Administration
Georgia State University
University Plaza
Atlanta, Georgia 30303

90 89 88 87   5 4 3 2

Georgia State University, a unit of the University System of Georgia, is an equal educational opportunity institution and equal opportunity/affirmative action employer.

Printed in the United States of America

Cover design by Marcia L. Lampe

TABLE OF CONTENTS

I
INTRODUCTION

Eric Kohler has been called one of the accounting giants of this century.[1] As a member of the American Accounting Association, he was a leader in the development of accounting principles, advocating a conceptual approach and insisting on careful communication and precise terminology in the articulation of standards. As editor of the <u>Accounting Review</u> and in other writings, he discussed such perennial issues as valuation and disclosure, stressing the importance of historical cost as the appropriate value for recording and reporting transactions and the importance of making financial statements readily understandable. Much of his career was devoted to governmental accounting, and as controller of the Tennessee Valley Authority and of the Economic Cooperation Administration (Marshall Plan), as well as as a consultant in the governmental area, he designed accounting systems which he believed would be responsive to the needs of each organization. He expressed concern that accounting education and research be designed to keep the profession a few steps ahead of the demands being placed on it at any point in time.

He wrote that accountants should face their professiona[l] responsibilities squarely, and he criticized vague o[r] ambiguous phraseology designed to protect the accountant[.] Such positions testify to the highly principled approac[h] which has been attributed to Kohler. He seems to hav[e] accepted the demands which such an approach made on him, an[d] he expected others to do the same. He has been described a[s] being firm in his advocacy of his beliefs, and, while such [a] position led to some well-publicized disagreements over th[e] years, it also seems to have gained him much respect in th[e] professional ranks. Because of these contributions, Eri[c] Kohler's influence on the development of accountancy bear[s] consideration.

The purpose of this monograph is to provide such a[n] examination. The study is based upon Kohler's writings[,] including published articles and books and personal papers[,] and upon correspondence and interviews with individuals wh[o] were acquainted with Kohler. The writings have been numerou[s] and diverse: published articles, speeches, and editorial[s] dealing variously with aspects of taxation, terminology[,] development of standards, and governmental accounting[;] textbooks in the areas of taxation, auditing, and financial[,] managerial, and governmental accounting; and, what is ofte[n] regarded as his major contribution, <u>A Dictionary fo[r] Accountants</u>.[2]

Additional insight into Kohler's thinking has been
obtained from unpublished materials housed in the Accounting
and Information Systems Department of the J. L. Kellogg
Graduate School of Management at Northwestern University.
These materials reinforce the ideas expressed in the
published works and include unpublished articles and speeches
as well as correspondence and other personal materials.

The following chapter first establishes the economic
and professional environment in the United States in the
early twentieth century, the environment in which the young
Eric Kohler began his accounting career. It is necessary to
have some understanding of this background in order to
appreciate and understand the development of his thought and
in order to place his ideas in the appropriate perspective.
Also useful to a fuller understanding of Kohler's place in
the development of accountancy is a knowledge of his own
background and the forces which shaped his character.
Chapter three, therefore, provides such biographical detail
as is relevant to a deeper understanding of Kohler's
philosophy of accounting.[3] The chapter also contains a brief
outline of some of the major tenets of that philosophy and
thus provides an indication of Kohler's major contributions.

Subsequent chapters focus on those contributions,
examining four areas which represent the primary emphases of
Kohler's writings. These are: (1) the development of
accounting principles, (2) the need for clear communication

fostered by precise terminology, (3) effective accounting for governmental agencies, and (4) the development of the profession. What emerges from the writings in each of these areas is an emphasis on simplicity, clarity, and comparability in the compilation and presentation of financial information and an overriding insistence on forthrightness, high principles, and a search for truth.

NOTES

[1]Robert K. Mautz and Gary John Previts, "Eric Kohler: An Accounting Original," Accounting Review (April, 1977), p. 307.

[2]The study emphasizes the theoretical writings, primarily the numerous articles and editorials, and A Dictionary for Accountants, and de-emphasizes the textbook writings. The textbooks, like textbooks in general, are primarily descriptive rather than prescriptive, and, as such, they offer less significant insight into Kohler's thought than do his other writings. Since the focus of the study is those areas to which Kohler remained committed throughout his lifetime, the early tax-related writings are also excluded.

[3]Eric Kohler was a very private person, and it has been noted that even those who knew him best did not know him well (See, for example, Mautz and Previts, above, p. 301). Therefore, no attempt is made to provide a psychological profile of Kohler or to identify explicitly those forces which motivated him. Some indication of his personality will emerge from the biographical sketch and, more importantly, from the discussion of his writings. However, any conclusions regarding motivating forces are outside the scope of the study.

II

ECONOMIC AND PROFESSIONAL ENVIRONMENT

THE ECONOMY

The early years of the twentieth century were a time of change in the American economy. The nation, which from its inception had been primarily agricultural, was now becoming a leader in industry. Its population, traditionally rural, was becoming increasingly urban and was being swollen by an influx of immigrants. The shifting, growing population, along with an abundance of natural resources and improved transportation and communication facilities, contributed to industrial expansion, providing a ready supply of labor and raw materials and the means of making materials and finished products available to consumers. Also contributing to industrial expansion was a continued close alliance between business and government. The era was a generally prosperous one, but extremes of wealth and poverty existed. The demand for economic, social, and political reform was growing, fueled and evidenced by the panic of 1893 and another panic in the securities markets in 1907; and government became a regulator of business. Nevertheless, investment in industry increased, financed by bank loans and wider issuance of securities, and the general feeling of prosperity of the era

5

also led to increased individual installment and credit buying. Such changes in the nation's economy set the stage for the growth of the accounting profession. The following section will present briefly the elements of change in the turn-of-the-century economy, including the growth of industry, the expanding population, improvements in transportation, the general prosperity of the era, the increasing role of government and the growing demands for corporate accountability.

Growth of Industry

Although farm products remained an important part of the American economy, the primary emphasis turned to manufacturing. The 1889 census reported that income from farm products had been outstripped by the value of manufactured goods,[1] signaling a trend in the nation's economy. In 1894 the United States for the first time ranked as the leader among the manufacturing nations of the world, and by 1914 manufacturing produced more of the country's private production income than did any other sector of the economy.[2] Although agricultural products continued to be a major part of the economic picture, by World War I the country's emergence as a major industrial power could no longer be questioned.

A Growing Population

The growing national population provided the factories and mines with sufficient labor to fuel their expanding power. The until-now predominantly rural population was becoming predominantly urban. By 1900 the number of individuals living in places with a population of 2,500 or more had grown to almost 40 percent, and by 1920 urban dwellers were a majority, constituting 51.4 percent of the population.[5] Many of these individuals were recent immigrants seeking greater opportunity. The migration, which after 1900 was primarily from southern and eastern Europe, by 1910 accounted for 14.5 percent of the population and for an even larger percentage (22.6%) of the urban population. Thus, individuals both from Europe and from the American farm migrated to the American city and thereby contributed to the changing character of the country's economy during the early years of the century.

The Railroads

Also contributing to rapid industrialization was the availability of transportation facilities. Financed by private investment, by assistance from state and local governments, and by federal land grants, railroads had by the early twentieth century become the most important form of transportation. They provided an efficient means for delivering the raw materials necessary to and the finished products resulting from the nation's industrial expansion. The railroads, controlled by 1906 primarily by four operational groups, were essential to the era's economy; thus tremendous power was held by a small number of individuals, and abuse of such power was perhaps inevitable. Charges of excessive profits and discriminatory practices led first to the Granger Laws in the 1870's and ultimately to the establishment of the Interstate Commerce Commission in 1887. Thus, although the railway system contributed indispensably to the industrialization and growth of the country, it also contributed importantly to a national discomfort which manifested itself in calls for reform and for greater government regulation.

Wealth and Poverty

The railroads were not the only cause of growing unrest. Although the post-Civil War era had been a generally prosperous one which witnessed a growing national wealth extremes of wealth and poverty existed. The agrarian-to-industrial shift contributed to enriching the few and impoverishing many for whom the promised opportunity of the urban, industrial areas turned to a harsh and uncomfortable reality. In an era in which the national wealth doubled and redoubled, increasing from $16 billion in 1860 to $88.5 billion in 1900 and over $186 billion in 1912 the wealthiest one percent of the population owned nearl half the wealth, and many families lived on only a few hundred dollars a year.[4] Declines in agricultural income, reduced wages, and worker discontent contributed to the panic of 1893, when loss of confidence in the monetary system and economic and social conditions in general triggered a run on banks and the failure of many businesses. The recovery from the resulting depression was a precursor to a long period of national prosperity, but it was a prosperity from which only a small percentage of Americans benefited. The stage was set for continued calls for economic, social, and political reform, and the federal government assumed an increasingly important role as a regulator of business.

Increasing Role of Government

Government, specifically the federal government, was becoming more important. By World War I it had gained prominence as an employer, a regulator, and a major source of national income. Traditionally a friend of business, government now responded to the public's demand for corporate accountability. In 1898 the Industrial Commission was formed and charged with investigating issues relating to immigration, labor, agriculture, manufacturing, and business. Many who testified before the Commission urged corporate publicity as a means of curbing abuses,[5] and in 1899 the New York Stock Exchange began to require financial statements on a regular basis from listed companies. These movements, along with the increasing number of mergers and acquisitions and expanded corporate ownership, provided a real impetus for the development of the accounting profession.

Demand for Greater Accountability

Financial statements at the beginning of the twentieth century were largely unrevealing and, in fact, were often deliberately designed to conceal.[8] Amid a tradition of secrecy and a fear of assisting competitors, the amount of information available for public consumption was small. Aggravating the problem was the fact that state laws and corporate charters provided few requirements for financial reporting. The result was documents such as that issued by the Board of Directors of Westinghouse Electric and Manufacturing Company in 1901. It was a two-page report containing no financial statements but giving sales, dividend, interest and sinking fund payments for 1898-1900. And in 1900 the American Tin Plate Company published a balance sheet which contained only four asset and five liability accounts. This brief report came from a company whose stock was publicly traded and which controlled 95 percent of the nation's tin plate production.[9] And, as long as the prevailing philosophy was that what was good for business was also good for the nation, such statements were not to be questioned. However, as demands for reform increased and as corporate ownership expanded, questions regarding the adequacy of such reports were raised, and the role and the responsibilities of the accounting profession expanded.

THE ACCOUNTING PROFESSION

At the turn of the century the accounting profession in the United States was in its formative stages, having just emerged from its struggle to pass the first Certified Public Accountant (CPA) laws and from several, often unsuccessful, attempts to establish accounting education at the college and university level. The national organization, the American Association of Public Accountants (AAPA), was less effective than the state organizations, particularly those in New York, Pennsylvania, and Illinois.[8] Efforts to establish a unified national organization were impeded by a continuing British-American rivalry and disagreements over appropriate requirements for membership and for professional certification. Amid charges that regulation was merely an unfair effort to restrict entry and that examinations were arbitrarily graded, there was a great deal of resistance to attempts to establish education, experience and examination requirements.

However, progress was being made. CPA legislation was being enacted: by 1914 twenty-nine states had passed CPA laws. In addition, accounting was becoming recognized as a legitimate field of study at the college and university level. The first International Congress of Accountants, held in St. Louis in 1904, was a step toward greater unity, bringing together as it did representatives of the AAPA, the Federation of Societies of Public Accountants in the United States, and the state societies, notably the New York State Society of Certified Public Accountants. The Journal of Accountancy, first established by the Illinois Society and called The Auditor, provided a national voice[9] and was another step toward professional growth.

This section will outline early efforts toward accounting legislation, education, and organization and will also deal briefly with conceptions of the accountant's role and thinking regarding certain basic accounting concepts.

The Formative Years: Recognition and Education

The first CPA law was passed in New York in 1896, a result of a two-year effort by the Institute of Accounts,[10] the American Association of Public Accountants, and public accountants belonging to neither organization. The act provided for licensing and examination as a prerequisite to use of the title CPA and also required U. S. citizenship, a requirement significant in view of the large British element of the accounting profession. This legislation was followed shortly by the passage of similar laws in Pennsylvania and Maryland; and, by the end of 1905, California, Illinois, Washington, New Jersey, Florida, and Michigan had followed suit.

A further step toward the development of a viable accounting profession was the establishment of educational programs and standards which would prepare the aspiring accountant for his role. Attempts to found a school of commerce had been made as early as 1851, but many of the early efforts were unsuccessful. The University of Louisiana abandoned its program in 1857, and the University of Illinois discontinued its School of Commerce in 1880. The New York School of Accounts, established in 1892 through the efforts of the AAPA, was abandoned in 1894. Among the successful efforts were the 1881 establishment of the Wharton School of Commerce and Finance, the first American collegiate school of business, and the establishment at New York University of the School of Commerce, Accounts and Finance, which contained the first department of accountancy as such. By 1900 thirteen universities and colleges offered accredited courses in accounting.

Instruction in these institutions was primarily technical and procedural, and textbooks were few; but the profession recognized the need to develop educational standards. At the 1906 AAPA meeting President Elijah Watt Sells stressed the importance of developing accounting education, and during the years 1908 to 1916 the organization's Committee on Education studied courses that were being taught, those the membership believed should be taught, and CPA requirements and methods of teaching. Developing educational programs and standards may, then, be seen to have been among the young profession's priorities.

The Formative Years: Professional Organization

A national organization, the American Association of Public Accountants, had been formed in 1887 in an effort to achieve broader recognition of the accounting profession. However, the organization was not acknowledged by accountants as one having national authority; and the state societies, particularly those in New York, Pennsylvania, and Illinois, were more influential than the national body.[11] It was through the efforts of the New York Society that New York University began its School of Commerce, Accounts, and Finance; and it was the Illinois Society that first published the periodical which became the Journal of Accountancy. Unfortunately, the effect of these separate efforts at professional development was to retard the development of a national unity.

An attempt to overcome the division was the formation in 1902 of the Federation of Societies of Public Accountants in the United States. However, because the Federation's goals clashed with those of the New York Society, the effort was less than successful, and in 1905 the Federation merged with the AAPA.

Although the profession, as a result of the merger, had a single national organization, it lacked national unity. Differences as to goals and priorities remained. Aggravating these internal divisions were other pressures: attempts to establish standards met with charges of monopolistic practices, of meaningless certification, and of capricious grading of CPA examinations. Accountants had to answer these charges if they were to respond effectively to the demands which accompanied the nation's industrial expansion.

The Accountant's Role

Primary among the profession's needs was a clear definition of the role of the public accountant. Was he artist or scientist? What was the nature of his obligation to management and to third parties? What should be the nature of the principles or standards which would govern his practice? Accountants were still far from agreeing on the answers to these questions.

The prevailing answer to the art-versus-science question seems to have been in favor of the accountant as artist. Some interpreted the accounting-as-science option as being synonymous with the imposition of narrow technical standards. When the Interstate Commerce Commission had instituted standard procedures for railroad reporting, CPA's had been replaced by technicians. It is understandable, then, that accounting professionals chose to emphasize expert guidance in the presentation of financial statements.

Professionals were less clear on their appropriate role in relation to management and to third parties. Some, like Kohler, contended that public accountants had profound social obligations and must assure that financial statements would not be misleading to third parties. Others, while professing a belief in obligations to third parties, clearly viewed their primary role as one of service to management. They saw the choice of accounting methods and procedures as a management option and considered the role of the accountant to be narrowly defined and limited to ascertaining the technical correctness of the account-keeping.[12]

Also unresolved was the question of the nature of standards. The general feeling seems to have been that standards must be broadly conceived, allowing ample room for the exercise of expert judgment. In the absence of prescribed standards, early practitioners viewed accountants as responsible for exercising judgment based on high ethical standards which condemned "acts discreditable to the profession" and was therefore responsive to investor needs. Pleas for uniformity were greeted skeptically, but pressure for more definitive standards continued. However, even had uniform standards been promulgated, no national organization had the authority to mandate compliance. Uniform Accounting,[13] published in 1917 and providing for wide areas of discretion, was frequently ignored by practitioners. It is apparent, then, that questions of uniformity, as well as others having to do with the accountant's role and responsibility, continued to be debated.

Basic Accounting Concepts

Accounting treatment of similar items varied widely, making financial statement interpretation difficult. One writer who reviewed about 150 corporate financial statements wrote of the lack of uniformity in the treatment of identical items, pointing to variations "sufficient to convert losses into profits, to alter materially the values assigned to important assets, and to render the several statements wholly noncomparable . . . ."[14] Nevertheless, certain basic characteristics can be identified.

First, it may be noted that the balance sheet assumed more importance than the income statement. The latter, in fact, was often viewed as merely an elaboration of one section of the balance sheet. Income determination was, then, not a primary concern, and the income statement was frequently viewed as a residual of the asset valuation process.

Second, consistency in asset valuation was absent from financial statements. Provisions for depreciation expense were frequently made in good years but ignored in bad ones, and pressure for recognition of appreciation increased during this period. The nature of the depreciation charge remained open to debate. Some contended that depreciation must represent an allocation of a past cost; others believed in the necessity of providing for depreciation charges sufficient to insure asset replacement.

Another frequent practice was the establishment of a reserve to transfer a portion of the earnings of prosperous years to less prosperous ones, the idea being that financial statements would, as a result, reflect more accurately the true earning power of the business enterprise. Such stabilization of earnings was accepted as good policy.[15] Of course, one means of providing for a smooth earnings flow was through charges to surplus accounts when a charge to income might result in a "distortion." Proper classification and definition of appropriate charges to surplus were, therefore, major problems which accompanied that of the presentation of a representative earnings picture.

SUMMARY

The accounting profession in the early years of the century was burdened with an abundance of unresolved problems: issues related to adequate legislation, education, and a viable organization were accompanied by questions regarding the accountant's role and the appropriate accounting treatment of financial statement items.

NOTES

[1] Gilbert C. Fite and Jim E. Reese, An Economic History of the United States (Boston: Houghton Mifflin Company, 1959), p. 289.

[2] Ibid., p. 304.

[3] Ibid., p. 301.

[4] Ibid., p. 307.

[5] Gary John Previts and Barbara Dubis Merino, A History of Accounting in America (New York: John Wiley and Sons, 1979), pp. 133-134.

[6] David F. Hawkins, "The Development of Modern Financial Reporting Practices Among American Manufacturing Corporations" in Contemporary Studies in the Evolution of Accounting Thought, Michael Chatfield, editor (Belmont, California: Dickenson Publishing Company, Inc., 1968), pp. 249-252.

[7] Ibid.

[8] Previts and Merino, p. 138.

[9] Ibid., p. 142.

[10] Ibid., pp. 93-94. The Institute of Accounts was a short-lived organization. Formed in New York in 1882 as the Institute of Accountants and Bookkeepers, it was the first professional accounting organization in the United States. It existed until about 1908 and numbered among its members Charles E. Sprague and Charles Waldo Haskins.

[11] Ibid., p. 138.

[12] John L. Carey, The Rise of the Accounting Profession: From Technician to Professional (New York: American Institute of Certified Public Accountants, 1969), p. 77.

[13] Federal Reserve Board, Uniform Accounting (Washington, D. C.: Government Printing Office, 1917).

[14] Howard C. Greer, "What Are Accepted Principles of Accounting?" Accounting Review (March, 1938), pp. 27-28.

[15] Previts and Merino, p. 181.

III

THE MAN AND HIS WORK: AN OVERVIEW

BIOGRAPHY

It was the environment just described which the young
Eric Louis Kohler entered upon his graduation from the
University of Michigan, where he received his Bachelor of
Arts degree in economics in 1914, and Northwestern
University, where he was granted a master's degree in
economics in 1915. Over the next sixty-one years, until his
death on February 20, 1976, Kohler was to have a significant
influence on the developing profession. He would encourage
accountants to establish an articulated set of accounting
principles, supported by a more precise terminology. He
would stress the importance of high ethical and professional
standards, accounting education, and research which is always
a few steps ahead of the demands of society. It was because
of such contributions that by the end of his career he would
have received the American Institute of Certified Public
Accountants Gold Medal and would have been inducted into the
Ohio State University Accounting Hall of Fame. It is also a
tribute to Kohler's impact on accountancy that he has been
memorialized by others of stature in the profession[1] and has

been called an accounting giant whose high standards helped to set the pace for the emerging accounting profession.[2]

Childhood and Education

Born in Owosso, Michigan, on July 9, 1892, to Kate Evelyn Bently Kohler and Frank Edwin Kohler, who was an Owosso dry goods merchant, Eric was the younger of two children. His brother, Frank, also became an accountant and, in fact, assisted Kohler in the preparation of some of his textbooks.[3] The high moral principles which Kohler exhibited throughout his career were instilled in a childhood home in which integrity, individualism, and high principles were emphasized.[4] Although Kohler considered his mother the major influence on his life, his father was "as much convinced of the need for integrity and high principles as Kohler ever was," and Kohler seems very much to have been affected by the father's attitudes.[5]

Neither Kohler nor his father were churchgoers, but both could be considered religious "in the deeper sense of holding very basic values which they regarded as controlling their lives."[6] Both were highly individualistic; "in fact, one of Kohler's favorite expressions was par ne rien que nous, which translates as "by nobody but ourselves."[7] This characteristic may help to explain his impatience with committees, especially when they required compromise.

An important childhood influence must have been

Kohler's high school principal, Durand W. Springer. An "intelligent, shrewd, thickskinned, and somewhat combative"[8] midwesterner, Springer was a leader in the American Society of Certified Public Accountants (ASCPA). His political instincts and exceptional energy made him an effective campaigner for the organization and an important factor in its rapid growth. His influence may help to explain Kohler's alliance with the ASCPA and his tendency to attribute all major professional contributions to that organization, even when the evidence clearly showed him to be incorrect.[9] Kohler, in fact, much later attributed to Springer "much of the push . . . given to a dormant profession into its hectic preoccupations of today."[10]

From Ann Arbor High School and Springer's influence, Kohler went on to the University of Michigan, where he intended to study journalism. He had spent two years as the Associated Press correspondent for sports in Ann Arbor and had other writing experience.[11] His undergraduate degree is, however, a B. A. in economics with an English literature minor.

When he received the degree in 1914, two or three individuals whom he respected suggested that he study at Northwestern University under Arthur Andersen. Kohler acted on their suggestion, received his master's degree in 1915, and began a long-term, though intermittent, association with Andersen.

Public Practice

Kohler was registered as a CPA in Illinois, Missouri, and Wisconsin. His association with Arthur Andersen & Co. began after his graduation from Northwestern. He practiced with the firm from 1915 to 1917, then served two years as a captain in the Quartermaster Corps during World War I and returned to the Andersen firm from 1919 to 1920.[12] Ultimately Kohler's individuality led him to establish his own practice: in 1922 he and another former member of the Arthur Andersen staff formed Kohler, Pettengill and Company. In 1928 Kohler formed E. L. Kohler and Company, became a member of the Illinois Board of CPA Examiners, and, most significantly, became editor of the Accounting Review, a post he would hold for nearly fifteen years.

Government Service

A Congressional inquiry into Tennessee Valley Authority activities resulted in Kohler's engagement as the Authority's controller in 1938. Kohler, who was charged with reorganizing the organization's accounting processes, brought in a team of independent auditors and secured the Authority's first unqualified report.[13] Kohler's subsequent testimony before a Joint Congressional Committee signaled the survival of the TVA and an ultimate overhaul of accounting procedure at the U. S. General Accounting Office.[14]

Kohler brought the same kind of administrative skills to his position ten years later as controller of the Economic Cooperation Administration (ECA) (Marshall Plan).[15] His public service also included his being a member of the staff of the Office of Emergency Management and War Production Board (1941-1942), an executive officer of the Petroleum Administration for War (1942-1944), and an accounting consultant both before and after his work with the ECA. He was financial advisor to the U. S. Secretary of Agriculture (1946), consultant to the U. S. General Accounting Office, and a member of the Advisory Panel on Organization of Congress. At the state level he was chairman of the Advisory Board to the Illinois Auditor General.

Professional Organizations

Kohler was a member of Beta Alpha Psi and its president from 1924 to 1927; and he was a member of Beta Gamma Sigma. In addition to his affiliation with the American Accounting Association (AAA), he was a charter member of the American Institute of Accountants and the American Institute of Certified Public Accountants. He was a member of the National Association of Accountants and the Illinois Society of Certified Public Accountants.

He became editor of the Accounting Review in 1928. During his nearly fifteen years in this position, he instituted an editorial page which he made his vehicle for

THE MAN AND HIS WORK/25

speaking out on matters of importance to accountants. As
Kohler recalled it, several of his articles and reviews were
"rather controversial in character; in fact, so controversial
in some cases that I was looked upon with some trepidation by
certain members of the profession."[16] He criticized the
profession for its complacency and challenged it to move
ahead to accept the demands which the future promised.

As a two-term president of the sponsoring organization
(1936 and 1946), the American Accounting Association, he
further extended his influence. He was, in fact, the first
president of the newly formed AAA when the American
Association of University Instructors in Accounting
reorganized and embraced a new and expanded set of
objectives. It was during Kohler's first term as AAA
president that the organization produced the "Tentative
Statement of Accounting Principles Affecting Corporate
Reports."[17]

In 1931 Kohler became a member of the American
Institute of Accountants (AIA) Committee on Terminology, and
he became chairman of that committee two years later. When
the Council rejected the committee's report and abolished the
committee, Robert Montgomery encouraged Kohler to continue on
his own, and A Dictionary for Accountants was conceived.
During this period Kohler returned to Arthur Andersen for an
additional four years (1933-1937) before entering a period of
government service.

Accounting Instruction

In 1922 Kohler became a professor in the evening School of Commerce at Northwestern University, joining the department headed by Arthur Andersen and also staffed by H. A. Finney. At the time accounting instruction was technique and procedure oriented, and Kohler's early textbooks, published during this period, reflect that orientation.[18] Kohler remained at Northwestern until 1928, the year he became editor of the Accounting Review.

Other academic activities included visiting professorships at American University (1941-44), Ohio State University (1955-60), the University of Minnesota (1955), the University of Chicago (1958) and the University of Illinois (1966).

Honors and Awards

In 1927 Kohler became the first accountant to be listed in Who's Who in America. In later years he received the AICPA Gold Medal for distinguished service (1948) and the Alpha Kappa Psi Foundation Accounting Award (1958). He was inducted into the Ohio State University Accounting Hall of Fame in 1961.

Other Interests

Kohler was a very private person, a lifelong bachelor interested in music, photography and electronics. His

interest in music began in his early years when he studied
music composition to prepare for a career as a composer and
critic.[19] He had intended in his college studies to become a
music critic and, when he went to Chicago to attend
Northwestern, he also enrolled in the American Conservatory
of Music, where he studied composition.[20] He continued to be
interested in music throughout his life and is said to have
discussed it with substantial knowledge.[21]

In later years he served as controller and advisor to
the Auditorium Theater Council of Chicago (1960-76). He was
a member of the Board of Trustees (1947-68) and of the
Advisory Council (1957-61) of the College of Business
Administration of Roosevelt Universisty. He also served as
president of the City Club of Chicago.

Aspects of His Personality

Something of Kohler's personality can be gleaned from
his appearance. His 6'4" frame towered over that of most of
his colleagues, and his angular features seemed to forewarn
one of his tenacity in holding to his positions. One
associate, Howard W. Wright, recalls their first meeting:

> A mutual friend arranged for Eric and me to have
> lunch. I walked into his office in downtown
> Washington for introductions. He started coming
> up from behind his desk and I thought that he
> would never stop. He held out his right hand
> and I thought he had a baseball glove on it.[22]

Others also point to Kohler as one who was "an impressive figure both physically and in the strength of his convictions."[23] His size seems to have contributed to his commanding the respect of his colleagues.

Eric Kohler was not one who would yield on matters of principle, and one of his associates has noted that the way to get Kohler seriously to consider a proposal was to identify one's recommendations with high moral precepts.[24] His commitment to such an approach is illustrated by an episode detailed by W. W. Cooper and Yuji Ijiri when he felt compelled to resign a post rather than yield on what he considered a matter of principle:

> Three very powerful U. S. senators requested an allocation of funds from this agency for a study which they believed was justified by its pertinence to the agency's mission, even though it had not been specifically allowed for in the budget. Kohler's required approval for this diversion of funds was not forthcoming, and so the matter was finally "bucked up" to the cabinet officer to whom the agency reported. Arguments such as "this kind of thing is done all the time" being of no avail, the cabinet officer finally ordered the requested diversion. Kohler promptly resigned.
> The agency head, an experienced high-level executive, followed Kohler back into his office to try to persuade him to withdraw his resignation. Finally, according to Kohler, this man said, "Look, Eric, you've been around. You're experienced enough to know that you have to get along with other people." "No, you don't," replied Kohler. "You have to get along with yourself." The agency head stopped. He looked Kohler squarely in the eye for a few moments. Then, as though for the first time appreciating the basic difference in principle that divided them, he dropped his voice and said to Kohler, "OK. I accept your resignation," and left the room.[25]

Those who knew him seem to remember most clearly Kohler's impressive presence, his serious demeanor, his vast knowledge of accounting, and his integrity and dedication to truth in accounting.[26]

An idealist, a man dedicated to truth and high principles, a man who tenaciously held to his opinions--these phrases seem to describe Eric Kohler. When such characteristics are combined with his vast business knowledge, his ability to perceive a problem and see it through to a practicable and principled solution, one can understand how he became a formidable force in the evolution of accounting thought in the United States.

The next section will detail some of the areas in which Kohler's influence was most strongly felt and will thereby provide an overview of chapters four through seven. These areas are: the development of accounting principles, which will be the subject of chapter four; the search for precise terminology, the subject of chapter five; accounting for government agencies, to be discussed in chapter six; and the accounting profession, its responsibilities and its problems, which will be the focus of chapter seven.

THE DEVELOPMENT OF ACCOUNTING PRINCIPLES

Eric Kohler was a leader in forging accounting principles, advocating a conceptual approach to the development of a small number of principles meant not as rules but as points of departure in situations requiring special treatment. Underlying his search for accounting principles is a dedication to truth and objectivity. An examination of Kohler's principles-related writings is best preceded by an understanding of his views regarding the purpose of accounting and the primacy of the transaction in fulfilling that purpose: accounting supplies orderly aid in the conduct of business; it furnishes information on financial position and operating results; it indicates the degree to which management has met its responsibility. Accounting achieves this purpose by classifying, recording, summarizing, and reporting transactions. Transactions are the only objective basis for valuation, recognition, and reporting. Chapter four contains an examination of the importance of the transaction in achieving accounting's purpose, the need for full disclosure, the importance of uniform standards, and the necessity of cost-based valuation.

Chapter four also provides an identification of Kohler's role in the development of the "Tentative Statement of Accounting Principles Affecting Corporate Reports" and, in the context of reviewing the propositions contained in that statement, it includes an examination of Koher's own views, as embodied in his other writings, of the issues in the three areas addressed by the Tentative Statement.

Kohler recognized the need for standards to provide

greater definition for the profession and to facilitate communication with outsiders. He criticized the American Institute of Accountant's (AIA) efforts at standards development, questioning the ability of those in public practice to see the larger picture clearly enough to contribute to the development of accounting theory.[27] He was convinced that the American Accounting Association (AAA) was the appropriate body to undertake the development of principles.

He has been identified as the leader of a group of dissatisfied members of the American Association of University Instructors in Accounting (AAUIA);[28] and he became the first president of the AAA, the organization which emerged from the AAUIA's struggle for redefinition. One of his first acts in this capacity was to draft a statement of principles which would provide a basis for appraising and constructing financial statements. The published "Tentative Statement of Accounting Principles Affecting Corporate Reports" addressed three problems which the AAA Executive Committee considered primary among current reporting difficulties: questions of (1) costs and value, (2) measurement of income, and (3) capital and surplus.[29] This statement and the events surrounding its writing are central to chapter four and provide a springboard for a discussion of Kohler's views in the three areas.

THE SEARCH FOR PRECISE TERMINOLOGY

Eric Kohler has been referred to as the arbiter of accounting definitions in recognition of the work for which he is most widely known: A Dictionary for Accountants. Although the first edition of the dictionary was not published until 1952, Kohler's lexicographic adventure began during his early professional years and became a lifelong occupation. He served on a committee to define earned surplus, chaired by Arthur Andersen, in 1929, and he later served on and chaired the American Institute of Accountants' Committee on Terminology. When that committee was abolished in 1937, he began his effort to "go it alone,"[30] and the dictionary began to take form. He seemed to view each edition as another draft, encouraging suggestions, contributions, and criticism, and engaging in continuous revision.

Kohler's developing interest in terminology is also evident in his writings from the very early ones forward. In 1926, for example, he urged accountants to adopt a standard terminology and classification and condemned the use of equivocal English to minimize liability.[31] He was especially critical of such emotional terms as "good accounting," "true income," or "best practice" and of such stopgap adjectives as acceptable, appropriate, proper, sound, and useful, claiming that such terms are freely interchangeable and are often employed so that one may avoid taking a position or so that the position taken remains vague enough to be acceptable to an entire committee. He saw careful definition as building the background for the introduction of logical principles.[32] The dictionary was, then, intended to provide a framework for the development of such principles.

Chapter five contains an examination of Kohler's commitment to improved terminology and its relationship to the development of accounting principles. It provides an identification of his work on the early terminology committees and his emerging and continuing effort to fight the terminological battle on his own. It includes a discussion of his criteria for accounting definitions and the areas in which he believed the accountant's language particularly fell short. Finally, it contains an examination of selected definitions in an effort to demonstrate Kohler's construction of the dictionary as a foundation for the development of accounting theory.

ACCOUNTING FOR GOVERNMENT AGENCIES

Much of Eric Kohler's professional life was devoted to accounting for government agencies. Perhaps he is best known in this regard for his years with the Tennessee Valley Authority as its controller. He also contributed to the success of the Marshall Plan (the Economic Cooperation Administration.)[33] In addition, he served as an administrator or consultant for several other government agencies.

In his writings in this area, certain themes are continuously repeated. Primary among these themes is the advocacy of an activity accounting system. Activity accounting is a responsibility accounting concept based on two fundamental ideas: (1) a person should not be held responsible for a cost over which he has no control, and (2) cost allocations and reallocations should, wherever possible, be avoided.[34] Another important theme is the role of the accountant as the public's representative in governmental fiscal matters. The accountant is responsible for creating standards in financing, budgeting, and expenditure controls. Specifically, the accountant should encourage governmental agencies to follow more closely the accounting practices of the private sector. He should discourage the booking of budgets and should encourage the adoption of responsibility accounting concepts and prompt, periodic reporting. He should advocate the installation of an extensive audit function which includes expenditure controls, routine examination of internal controls and accounting procedures, and periodic audits by public accountants. A final recurring theme is the separation of accounting and management. One cannot, Kohler said, create a well-run organization simply by requiring certain bookkeeping devices. Accounting provides the means to make management control possible, but the ultimate responsibility rests with qualified managers.

Chapter six contains an examination of Kohler's role as controller of the Tennessee Valley Authority, particularly his installation of an activity accounting system for that organization. It includes a discussion of his views on accounting within other governmental agencies, views which build on the conviction that there is no compelling reason why accounting in the public sector should differ in any meaningful way from accounting for private business enterprises. Finally, the chapter provides a discussion of Kohler's views on the separation and interrelationship of accounting and management.

THE PROFESSION

Kohler wrote frequently about the accounting profession, the goals for which he felt it should strive and the responsibilities which he felt it should embrace. In a March, 1931, Accounting Review editorial, he summarized the profession's research problems as falling into two categories: social and internal. The social problems are those having to do with the accountant's duty and responsibility to society; the internal problems relate to ethics, education, and a body of theory which remains a few steps ahead of society's demands. He condemned accountants for failing to do their own thinking and for relying on attorneys to tell them how far their responsibility extended.[35] He deplored phraseology in the audit report which, he believed, was designed not to inform the reader but to protect the accountant; and he called on the profession to raise the level of honesty and fair practice in business.[36] He believed that good practice, based on acceptance of this responsibility and upon a constant research effort aimed at the development of sound theory, could then become classroom material, capable of being analyzed and assimilated and thus providing the basis for the ongoing development of the profession. The goal of accounting education, as Kohler saw it, was to go beyond a "well-ordered collection of procedures" and to broaden the concept and usefulness of the accountant's role.[37] Augmenting the contribution of education would be a continuous research program on the part of professionals, especially academics.

Accountants' liability, education, and research must all be discussed in the context of the social implications of the accountant's art. Both theory and procedure, according to Kohler, must be formulated "with society itself as the background and the good of society as the objective."[38] Of course, he recognized that, if the accountant accepts his responsibilities on the terms suggested, he will have to recognize increased obligations. However, these obligations are no less than those that would be accepted by a profession whose high principles would mirror Kohler's own: a dedication to truth, integrity, and service to society.

Chapter seven provides an exploration of Kohler's views

on responsibilities of the profession: the external responsibilities to society and the internal structure--education and research--which will contribute to the fulfillment of the social obligation.

SUMMARY

This chapter has provided the biographical setting for an exploration of Kohler's role in the development of accounting thought. It has also provided a brief indication of the contributions to be explored in subsequent chapters. The areas to be examined are: the search for accounting principles, the concern for precise terminology, the role of accounting in the public sector, and the responsibilities of the accounting profession. In each of these areas, Kohler's thought gives evidence of a search for clear definition of standards, terms, and responsibilities and for complete and truthful representation. The standards which he set for himself and for the profession were consistently high, earning him the title "accounting's man of principles."[39]

NOTES

[1]For example, see W. W. Cooper and Yuji Ijiri, Eric Louis Kohler: Accounting's Man of Principles (Reston, Virginia: Reston Publishing Company, 1979); James Don Edwards and Roland F. Salmonson, Contributions of Four Accounting Pioneers (East Lansing, Michigan: Michigan State University Business Studies, 1961); W. W. Cooper, Yuji Ijiri, and Gary John Previts, editors, Eric Louis Kohler: A Collection of his Writings (1919-1975) (Atlanta, Georgia: The Academy of Accounting Historians, 1980); and Robert K. Mautz and Gary John Previts, "Eric Kohler: An Accounting Original," Accounting Review (April, 1977).

[2]Mautz and Previts, p. 307.

[3]As indicated in the prefaces to Advanced Accounting Problems, Second Edition; Principles of Accounting, First Edition; and Auditing: An Introduction to the Work of the Public Accountant, Second Edition.

[4]The early biographical material related in this section is based on an interview with W. W. Cooper, Foster Parker Professor of Finance and Management at the University of Texas at Austin. Cooper is widely regarded as being the foremost authority on Kohler's life and thought and was closely associated with Kohler in connection with the "Tentative Statement of Accounting Principles Affecting Corporate Reports," the Dictionary for Accountants, the Tennessee Valley Authority, and the Economic Cooperation Administration, as well as in other capacities.

[5]Interview with W. W. Cooper. It is interesting to note that, although Eric Kohler was considered quite tall for a man of his time (6'4"), his father stood something under 5'8".

[6]Interview with W. W. Cooper.

[7]Ibid.

[8]John L. Carey, "The CPA's Professional Heritage, Part I," in Accounting Historian's Working Papers, Volume I (Atlanta, Georgia: The Academy of Accounting Historians, 1975), p. 6.

[9]Gary John Previts and Barbara Dubis Merino, A History of Accounting in America (New York: John Wiley and Sons, 1979), p. 207.

[10]Eric L. Kohler, "In All My Years," The Accounting Historian (Spring, 1975), p. 6.

[11]Eric L. Kohler, Tennessee Valley Authority Oral History (Memphis, Tennessee: Memphis State University Oral History Research Office, February, 1971), p. 2.

[12]Thomas J. Burns and Edward N. Coffman, The Accounting Hall of Fame: Profiles of Thirty-Six Members (College of Administrative Science, The Ohio State University, 1976), p. 31.

[13]Jerry F. Stone, "Eric L. Kohler, Comptroller of the Tennessee Valley Authority (1938-1941)" in Eric Louis Kohler: Accounting's Man of Principles, W. W. Cooper and Yuji Ijiri, editors, p. 88. The report did contain an exception regarding allocations related to the interpretation of the Tennessee Valley Authority Act.

[14]Ibid., and William W. Cooper and Walter F. Frese, "Turnaround at the GAO" in Eric Louis Kohler: Accounting's Man of Principles, pp. 127-156.

[15]Samuel Nakasian, "Eric Kohler in the Marshall Plan," in Eric Louis Kohler: Accounting's Man of Principles, pp. 98-113.

[16]Kohler, TVA Oral History, p. 6.

[17]"A Tentative Statement of Accounting Principles Affecting Corporate Reports," Accounting Review (June, 1936), pp. 187-191.

[18]These include two taxation textbooks--Accounting Principles Underlying Federal Income Taxes (1924) and Federal Income Taxes (1927)--and two principles texts--Principles of Accounting, with Paul L. Morrison, a finance instructor at Northwestern (1926) and Principles of Auditing by Kohler with his associate, Paul W. Pettengill. The first of these principles texts was at least partially based upon Kohler's preparation to teach for the first semester course in accounting at Northwestern and was then expanded to cover the year's work. In addition, it was during his tenure at Northwestern that Kohler wrote Accounting for Business Executives, a primer to give the executive some understanding of the accountant's art.

[19]Cooper and Ijiri, p. viii.

[20]Interview with W. W. Cooper.

[21]Letter from Howard W. Wright. According to Wright, one outgrowth of Kohler's interest in music was that he made hi-fi sets which he gave to public institutions so that the residents could enjoy classical music.

[22]Ibid.

[23]Letter from Andrew Barr. Mautz and Previts also note that "Kohler's impressive height and serious demeanor added to the impact of his presence at professional meetings," p. 304.

[24]Nakasian, p. 101.

[25]Cooper and Ijiri, p. 11. Reprinted by permission of Prentice-Hall, Inc., Englewood Cliffs, New Jersey.

[26]Letters from Wright, Barr, Robert Dickey, Herbert Miller; see also Mautz and Previts.

[27]Eric L. Kohler, "Convention Report: Business Meeting of the Association," Accounting Review (March, 1937), p. 71.

[28]Howard C. Greer, "Benchmarks and Beacons," Accounting Review (January, 1956), p. 5.

[29]"Tentative Statement," p. 187.

[30]Kohler, "In All My Years," p. 4.

[31]Eric L. Kohler, "Tendencies in Balance Sheet Construction," Accounting Review (December, 1926), p. 3.

[32]Eric L. Kohler, "Some Principles for Terminologists," Accounting Review (March, 1935), pp. 31-33.

[33]See Nakasian.

[34]Stone, p. 90.

[35]Eric L. Kohler, "A Nervous Profession," Accounting Review (December, 1934), p. 334.

[36]Eric L. Kohler, "Audit Extensions," Accounting Review (September, 1939), p. 320.

[37]Eric L. Kohler, "The Goal of Accounting Education," Experiences with Extensions of Auditing Procedure (American Institute of Accountants, 1940-41), p. 88.

[38]Eric L. Kohler, "Research Problems," Accounting Review (March, 1931), p. 81.

[39]Cooper and Ijiri, p. 3.

IV
DEVELOPMENT OF ACCOUNTING PRINCIPLES

Eric Kohler has been called accounting's man of principles both because he was a highly principled man and because he was instrumental in the development of accounting principles. His high principles, in fact, underlie his approach to the development of standards: "The accountant is bound to tell the truth," he stated. "If the truth hurts, should it be glossed over?"[1] His answer is a resounding <u>no</u>. Through the development of standards, the profession provides greater assurance that the truth will not be glossed over.

This chapter contains an examination of Kohler's statement of the purpose of accounting and the primacy of the transaction in achieving that purpose. It includes a brief exploration of the positions that follow logically from this view: the need for full disclosure, uniform standards, and valuation based on historical cost. It provides an examination of Kohler's role in the development of accounting principles, including his leadership in the formulation of "A Tentative Statement of Accounting Principles Affecting Corporate Reports," which was published by the American

Accounting Association (AAA) in June, 1936. The chapter contains a review of the historical and professional context in which the statement developed and recounts the basic propositions presented in the four-and-a-half-page document. In that context it contains a more detailed exploration of Kohler's own views in each of the primary areas addressed by the statement: (1) costs and value, (2) measurement of income, and (3) capital and surplus. Finally, it includes a discussion of his role in later AAA principles-related projects. From this examination an appreciation of Kohler's role in the development of accounting principles emerges.

THE PURPOSE OF ACCOUNTING

One may develop a greater appreciation for Kohler's principles-related writings by first examining his statement of the purpose of accounting. That purpose is threefold. First, accounting supplies orderly aid in the conduct of business. It is the language in which management does much of its thinking and communicating.[2] It provides management with an instrument for internal control over the enterprise's policies and operations.[3] Second, accounting furnishes information on financial position and operating results. Thus, accounting provides a service for external as well as internal users, and in this connection it fulfills the third part of its purpose: accounting indicates the degree to which management has met its responsibility. Accounting, then, not only becomes a useful tool for business management but also fulfills an important obligation to third persons. It is in the recognition of this obligation to society as a whole that the accountant merits the title <u>public</u> accountant and becomes responsible for developing accounting principles which promote the supplying of complete and objective information.

THE TRANSACTION

Accounting achieves its purpose by classifying, recording, summarizing, and reporting <u>transactions</u>. The transaction is primary among Kohler's primitives, or building blocks of accounting. As he stated it, "Transactions are the raw material of accounting."[4] They provide the only truthful, i.e., objective, basis for valuation, recognition, and ultimate reporting and, as such, constitute the essence of accounting methodology.

THE QUEST FOR PRINCIPLES

Kohler's transactions-based approach and dedication to truth and high principles underlie his quest for accounting principles. Because he believed that the accountant has an obligation to the public, he emphasized the need for financial statements which reveal rather than conceal.[5] Because he recognized human weakness and the power exerted by the need to make a showing, he urged uniform standards.[6]

Because he believed strongly in the primacy of the transaction as supplying the basis for truthful, objective accounting information, he was a staunch advocate of historical cost-based valuation.[7] These beliefs supplied his foundation for standards development.

Reveal, Not Conceal

"Every balance sheet," Kohler said, "should be crowded with information."[8] He abhorred the presentation of uninformative financial statements. He was convinced that statements should be understandable to the individual with only limited business experience and expressed the fear that corporate reports were often unintelligible even to many accountants. Inadequate disclosure, along with imprecise terminology and lack of uniformity, is to be blamed. Reports are, in fact, often only glowing advertisements, subordinating facts to such adornments as pretty typing and a gold seal.[9] He blasted condensed balance sheets and the descriptive balance sheets of some utilities, calling them "soupy pablum" and complaining that they belabor the obvious and leave the ordinary reader totally mystified about the important items.[10]

He listed six requirements for the intelligible all-purpose balance sheet: (1) It must assume an intelligent reader whose response to full disclosure will be positive and sympathetic; (2) It must supply maximum information for interpretive purposes; (3) It must group balance-sheet items under descriptive headings; (4) It must provide ready information on the face of the balance sheet regarding the valuation of all assets; (5) It must readily identify assets pledged to secure liabilities; and (6) It must reflect details of changes in funded debt and net worth.[11] These are a minimum. In short, all important information must be readily at hand, preferably on the face of the statement.

Uniformity

Among the primary reasons for uninformative financial statements is the lack of uniform standards. As a member of the American Society of Certified Public Accountants (ASCPA) Committee on Technical Affairs in 1929, Kohler called for the creation of an agency to establish uniform procedures, and in a 1931 article he pointed out that current practice had reached the point that it was both desirable and possible to codify certain fundamental principles.[12] In order to facilitate communication and minimize manipulation, the profession, he believed, must develop standards which would lead to greater uniformity in the treatment of identical or similar items. Only through the establishment of such standards could the purpose of accounting be achieved.

This viewpoint was not universally popular. Many accountants feared that uniform standards would rob them of a necessary flexibility and cloak them in a straitjacket of rules. They cited their status as professionals, not mere technicians, and pointed out that the application of uniform standards might imply to investors a greater degree of assurance than actually existed. They stressed the limitations of audits and the character of financial statements as expressions of management opinion.[13] The complexities of the business world, after all, proscribed uniform standards. Kohler was impatient with much of this thinking. While he recognized that the imposition of a rule book was neither possible nor desirable, he was nevertheless convinced that the profession had reached the point that some greater standardization was necessary. He argued that the mere attempt to formulate standards would eliminate many inconsistencies, and he believed that, unless some uniformity existed, there was too much opportunity for compromise in the name of expediency or convenience.

Objectivity

Were accountants of a vision transcending that of mere mortals, were they dedicated unequivocably to the pursuit of the greatest good for all men, then uniform standards might not be necessary and valuations other than historical cost might be appropriate.[14] But, since other numbers are, in Kohler's view, highly subjective, even arbitrary, and since they represent a departure from the function of accounting, which is to record, summarize, and report transactions, valuation based on amounts other than historical cost is inappropriate. Such valuation muddles communication and invites manipulation. When the introduction of other than cost-based information is necessary, as it may be in management decision making, he proposed forward accounting. Forward accounting fulfills management's need to look ahead and includes standard costs, budgeting procedures, breakeven charts, and estimates of cash requirements and cash positions. Historical cost is, however, the only defensible basis for external reporting.

THE NEED FOR STANDARDS

In 1934 corporate reporting, and with it the accounting profession, was under fire, apparently with good cause. Financial statements of the time lacked uniformity and seemed often to depend on managerial whim. Until the passage of the Securities Act of 1933 and the Securities Exchange Act of 1934, corporate statements were sketchy, a holdover from past emphasis on corporate secrecy; and, in deference to creditors, conservatism was the rule of the day. Added to these problems was the charge that accountants were being influenced less by their responsibility to the public than by management's desire to make a showing.[15] Treatment of the same or highly similar items varied widely, and the Securities and Exchange Commission (SEC) found itself in a quandary. Having been charged with deciding whether registrants were following accepted accounting procedures, Carman Blough, SEC Chief Accountant, complained, "It is almost unbelievable how many times questions are presented upon which it is impossible to find uniformity of opinion among textbook writers or among practicing accountants." He urged accountants to accept their increasing responsibilities to the public and to develop a uniform approach.[16]

Kohler echoed this concern in his Accounting Review editorials, using his position as editor to prod accountants into action. His strongest statement of impatience with the profession's smug, self-satisfied approach was his December, 1934, editorial, "A Nervous Profession." Therein he attacked accountants for their continued failure to recognize the problems at hand and to take positive and definite action to set standards for themselves. Only through the imposition of such standards could accountancy indicate the boundaries which distinguish it from related fields, provide discipline for those within the boundaries, and provide guidance for those who have dealings with members of the profession.[17]

"A Nervous Profession" was not Kohler's first such criticism. In 1931, for example, he had described both accounting theory and practice as "drifting aimlessly and needlessly on our uncertain and much disturbed sea of economic endeavor," and he pointed out that the accountant must become the determiner of financial standards lest others impose standards on the profession.[18] Carman Blough warned professionals that this prophecy could well be fulfilled when he told the American Institute of Accountants (AIA) that wide differences in accounting for similar transactions were not acceptable and that, if the profession itself did not take corrective measures, the SEC had both the authority and the willingness to do so. The need for standards was clear.

Kohler's conviction that standards were essential and the sort of opposition he faced are illustrated in a 1935 piece entitled "Standards: A Dialogue."[19] In that writing, he presents Bardley, a fictional accounting professor, and MacMurdie, also fictional, a practitioner born and educated abroad. Bardley's pleas for greater standardization are countered by MacMurdie's statements that the complexities of the business world make such uniformity impossible. Financial statements, MacMurdie explains, are, after all, expressions of judgment by management, and the accountant has little right to interfere with that judgment. His duty extends only to qualifying his certificate if the statement "appears too sour." He continues that the formulation of standards is hardly a proper occupation for a national organization of accountants. The organization, MacMurdie says, is better directed toward getting professionals together to behave as gentlemen toward one another. Kohler's criticism of the AIA seems clear in his portrayal of MacMurdie. Bardley, on the other hand, echoes Kohler's own sentiments and believes that standards are necessary as an aid in the definition of rules of ethics, as a means whereby the public can examine and know what to expect from accountants, and as a basis on which the profession can grow. It seems evident that the reader is meant to conclude that there is a demonstrated need for greater standardization.

RESPONSE TO THE NEED FOR STANDARDS

AIA Response

The American Institute of Accountants responded to the threat of federal intervention by appointing the Committee on Coooperation with Stock Exchanges. The AIA's publication in 1934 of Audits of Corporate Accounts provided evidence, in the eyes of members of that organization, that the profession could on its own develop accounting principles.[20] This pamphlet contained correspondence between the Institute's committee and the Committee on Stock List of the New York Stock Exchange. It clarified the auditor's responsibility, introduced the concept of generally accepted accounting principles and of consistency in their application from year to year, and presented a standard form for the auditor's report.[21] With this publication the Institute believed that it was making progress in establishing accounting principles.

Kohler was not convinced. In the same pages in which he criticized the AIA for its smugness and complacency, however, he commended Audits of Corporate Accounts, crediting George O. May with having revealed certain limitations and weaknesses in the profession and with having taken a step toward more responsible reporting. But he questioned whether disclosure without more than the meagre standardization indicated was sufficient.

Other Institute works did not fare so well in Kohler's view. He looked at the work of the Committee on Development of Accounting Principles and concluded that its recommendations, which paralleled those of Audits of Corporate Accounts, were superficial and lacking in a sound approach to an urgent problem.[22] In general, he found the Institute's efforts inadequate and questioned the ability of practitioners to see the larger picture clearly enough to develop the necessary standards.

AAA Response

Having despaired of the ability of the Institute to provide the profession with a much-needed, well-articulated set of accounting principles, Kohler called on the American Association of University Instructors in Accounting (AAUIA) to act.

Reorganization of the AAUIA

Kohler has been identified as the leader of a group of dissatisfied AAUIA members who wished "to make this association a positive force for the development of sound principles for the accounting expression of facts of business life."[23] As early as 1923, he, along with William A. Paton and Howard C. Greer, was active in pushing for change within the young organization. Research and theory began to be emphasized during this time, and in 1924 the Association amended its constitution to reflect the expanding orientation. However, four years later no real effort to act on the new objectives had surfaced.

Kohler made other attempts. When he became editor of the Accounting Review in 1928, he began to use an editorial page to prod the Association and the profession into action. In 1931 he became chairman of a Committee on Accounting Research and Education, a joint project of the AAUIA and the ASCPA. It was as chairman of this committee that he presented his "Research Plan for Accountancy," calling for at least a ten-year research program; and in 1931 a Council on Accounting Research was formed to plan such a program. However, the depression intervened, interest waned, and no positive steps for change were taken.

Finally, at the December, 1935, AAUIA meeting, he was one of several Association members who again urged change, and, as he described it, "action became the order of the day."[24] The Association changed its name to the American Accounting Association, extended membership to the practicing profession and other interested individuals, and adopted broader-ranging objectives, including: "to encourage and sponsor research in accounting" and "to develop accounting principles and standards, and to seek their endorsement or adoption by business enterprises, public and private accountants, and governmental bodies."[25] The AAA had made a commitment to becoming a positive force in the development of accounting principles.

The Tentative Statement

With Kohler as the new organization's president, the first order of business was a charge to a five-man Executive Committee to draft "principles on which financial statements could be based, and which might stand some chance of general acceptance."[26]

The Executive Committee assigned to Kohler the task of writing the first draft of a statement which would meet these criteria. Thus began a three-month effort to develop standards along the lines Kohler had, for years, been advocating.

The goal was expressed in a March, 1936, statement of objectives of the AAA: there should be a clear, consistent body of principles to which a set of financial statements might be said to conform. These principles should be intelligible to the layman who is acquainted with business affairs. They should not demand rigid uniformity but should constitute an explanation of what financial statements purport to signify.[27] The committee described its effort as an "experimental formulation of principles,"[28] designed as a step in achieving greater uniformity in the presentation of corporate reports and moving toward the presentation of those reports in conformity with a unified theory of accountancy. The committee recognized that, because business enterprises are so diverse, no single set of "rules" would ultimately be workable. It believed, however, that some greater uniformity based on standards of adequacy and reasonableness, could be found. Its conviction as stated was that

> it should still be possible to agree upon a foundation of underlying considerations which will tend to eliminate random variations in accounting procedure resulting not from the peculiarities of individual enterprises, but rather from the varying ideas of financiers and corporate executives as to what will be expedient, plausible or persuasive to investors at any given point in time.[29]

The foundation which was then set forth attempted to identify the primary sources of random variation and to move toward more consistent treatment in these areas of difficulty.

The propositions outlined in "A Tentative Statement of Accounting Principles Affecting Corporate Reports" addressed what the committee believed were primary among current reporting difficulties. The propositions were twenty in number but have been reduced to three major categories or underlying ideas:

> (1) Accounting is essentially a process of cost allocation rather than one of valuation.
>
> (2) The all-inclusive concept of income should be applied in financial reporting.
>
> (3) A clear distinction should be maintained between paid-in capital and retained earnings.[30]

The statement did not simply reflect current practice. For example, neither the all-inclusive concept of income nor the proposed treatment of unamortized discount on bonds were generally accepted. Of course, the work was never intended simply to reflect current practice. In fact, its framers recognized that it would inevitably conflict with practice since accounting practice at the time already embodied numerous conflicts; they wished only to avoid conflict with existing law and to produce a document useful to business, government, and investors.[31]

Of course, it is difficult to separate the parts of a committee effort and to identify the contributions of each individual. It is, however, interesting to examine the propositions of the Tentative Statement in relation to Kohler's solo writings and to compare the ideas there expressed with those espoused by the Executive Committee. The similarities could, of course, merely testify to the thought prevailing among the group as a whole, but this explanation seems unlikely. Howard Greer has, in fact, indicated that the committee did not easily agree: "If you think it isn't a task to bring together the conflicting opinions of people like Paton, Littleton, Kohler and Greer, you underrate their abilities to disagree with each other."[32] An examination of other writings of the individuals involved provides further testimony to their areas of disagreement.

An examination of Kohler's writing, then, may provide an indication of the depth of his influence in the drafting of the committee's statement.

Costs and value

The Tentative Statement's first seven propositions, grouped under the heading of "costs and values," define valuation as a process of allocating costs to current and future periods. Value information other than cost is relegated to supplementary notes. Adjustment for ordinary price-level changes is deemed unnecessary, and other adjustments based on expected business developments or appraisals are likewise viewed as unsatisfactory. Only cost-related records are conducive to meaningful financial interpretation.

Reporting on transactions. Kohler agreed with these propositions. He has been identified as a firm advocate of cost-based valuation. His conviction that such a position provides the only sound basis for reporting stems from his belief that the pivotal point for all accounting is the transaction. The accountant is concerned with auditing, recording, classifying, and reporting on transactions. The balance sheet presents "the status of transactions that provide the carryover into the next period's financial activities"; the income statement presents "a display of concluded transactions that make up the past period's profit or loss."[33] Every item is made up of transactions; financial statements report management's administration of the transaction process.[34]

Price, reflected in arm's-length transactions with outsiders, is the proper basis for valuation. By reflecting actual transactions, cost provides an indication of the way management has met its responsibilities. The use of price indices, on the other hand, results in confusion and opens the door to various manipulative practices.[35] This, in essence, is the Kohler position: historical-cost-based valuation provides an objective, clear-cut means of communicating with financial statement users.

Reflecting replacement cost. To assume that the ultimate replacement of an asset is a part of its present cost is fallacious.[36] To include such values in financial statements impedes their function as a reflection of management stewardship. Is not management performance better described, Kohler asks, by reporting original costs and the economies these costs have made possible?[37]

Replacement cost is also an inappropriate basis for charges for property exhaustion. Assets should be stated at original cost, and cost expirations should be based on a straight-line allocation of these past costs. Prospective adjustments may be necessary if original estimates of useful life prove inaccurate; and, while write-downs may sometimes be justified, restorations of asset value cannot. Cost allocations such as amortization have been made according to a carefully considered plan. To reverse these decisions in later years is to attack the integrity of the earlier financial statements.[38]

Applying index numbers. The use of index numbers to adjust asset values for inflation is also condemned. One who records fixed assets at cost is not necessarily assuming a stable monetary unit. Nor is he adding apples and oranges. He is instead reflecting the acquisition of the assets at a variety of price levels. Management performance is best measured in records and reports based on original cost. Management cannot, after all, be held responsible for price-level increases.

Moreover, the application of index numbers can actually contribute to inflation. Kohler contended that the current value adjustments of the 1920s actually contributed to, rather than merely reflected, inflation.[39] Furthermore, soaring prices represent an unstable and temporary development, and to give recognition to price changes is to introduce an unacceptable instability into the financial statements.[40]

Finally, Kohler asked how the appropriate value would be determined. Conditions attaching to a particular business enterprise are so unique that the application of an index number, representing as it does an average, is really worthless.[41] Moreover, if the adjustment depends on management judgment, the door to manipulative practices is opened.

Advocating historical cost. From the Tentative Statement and before, Kohler argued that accounting is not a process of valuation but of cost allocation. Years later he repeated the historical cost endorsement of the 1936 document and expressed his conviction that this position had never been seriously or convincingly challenged. The challenge to which he was specifically responding was that presented by the proposals of the American Institute of Certified Public Accountants' (AICPA) Accounting Research Studies One and Three. He viewed these revaluation proposals as presenting no real threat to the traditional historical cost orientation. In fact, he said that evidence presented in these studies left him more than ever convinced of the superiority of historical cost as the basis for recording and reporting asset values.[42] And he repeated his reasons, which he had given over the years, for clinging steadfastly to historical cost. His arguments may be summarized as follows:

   1. Historical cost, by reflecting actual transactions, indicates to stockholders and the public the manner in

which management has met its responsibilities.

2. No reliable general index for accurate adjustment exists. Use of a series of specific indices, on the other hand, would create a "hodgepodge of valuations" that would confuse management, stockholders, and analysts. Furthermore, such subjective valuations give management more opportunity to choose an approach that will place them in the best possible, but not necessarily most revealing, light.

3. Because of technological advances, many fixed assets have been recently acquired. Hence, their actual costs, like most inventory costs, are little different from their replacement costs.

4. Arguments for revaluation have failed to provide a convincing case that such adjustments result in a real benefit to stockholders and management.

5. Footnote disclosure is a sufficient and preferable means of providing such value-related information.

6. The recording of current values can actually contribute to inflation.

7. The argument that price-level adjustment provides more uniform valuation is based upon the idea that such a mixture of unit prices violates some logical

principle. This argument is without substance since accountants already use average costs.[43]

Forward accounting. Finally, Kohler proposed forward accounting as a means of giving appropriate and useful information regarding values other than cost. Forward accounting looks to the future and employs any basis of valuation conducive to the decision-making process. It includes standard costs, budgeting procedures, break-even charts, and estimates of cash requirements and cash positions. Forward costs anticipate situations which lie ahead and are expected to modify current operating patterns. They are subjective, reflecting management judgments, projections, and directives. Under forward accounting techniques, fixed assets, for example, could be assigned whatever value their contribution to the production process might justify.[44]

Measurement of income

The next six propositions of the Tentative Statement center on the all-inclusive income statement. The overall objective in the measurement of income, according to the statement, is to provide "a common yardstick" which reflects not only revenues and expenses of the current operating period but also those gains and losses recognized in but not strictly applicable to the period.[45] This basis for income measurement was not generally accepted in 1936 and, in fact, the AIA's Committee on Accounting Procedure opted for the current operating approach. In addition to its advocacy of an all-inclusive income statement, the AAA Executive Committee condemned the practice of creating reserves in order to artificially stabilize or smooth income over a number of periods; and charges to surplus were ruled out.

A historical summary. Again Kohler's writings agree. The income statement, he contended, should be a historical summary reflecting all expenses and losses.[46] He criticized the AIA's expedient approach that, although it is desirable to charge all expenses and losses against income, such treatment represents a theoretical ideal that is not always attainable. The Institute committee's position seemed to be that, if charges to income resulted in a distortion of current earnings, charges to earned surplus were permitted. Kohler's complaint was that what consituted a distortion of earnings had not been specified; therefore, management was free to charge all but the smallest losses to surplus on the basis that to include such items in the determination of income would create a distortion. References to "sound" methods or "distortions" of "earning power" he found vague, and he believed that they left management free to do whatever it wanted. Earning power, he argued, depends on hazards and contingencies outside the accountant's area of expertise.

Each income statement must be recognized as one of a series reflecting the results of operations and containing every item of expense or loss. No one statement, no matter how carefully prepared, can serve as an index of earning power. The better approach is, therefore, to provide a detailed summary of what has happened during the year and to disclose the primary historical variables.[47]

Kohler was critical of practices which manipulate the income statement to insure that there is always a net profit appearing on the bottom line. These practices include charges to surplus which relieve the current income account of embarrassment and the creation of reserves designed to stabilize the income picture over a period of years. His commitment to truth and a fair and complete presentation led him to ask:

> Would not business be more healthy if it would take the losses, if its leaders would face their stockholders with all the facts, and encourage accountants to adopt uniform standards for financial statements and reports rather than coerce them into accepting dubious measures for the purpose of "making a showing."[48]

Among the dubious measures which, he contended, distort the income picture are the adoption of LIFO or accelerated depreciation or the application of index numbers. The purpose of income determination, he said, is to portray past transactions and not to provide for future ones.[49] Therefore, income accounting must be cost-based, matching historical costs against revenues.

One of the measures which he criticized was the adoption of the last-in-first-out method of inventory valuation. "One does not buy tomorrow what he sells today," he complained;[50] and he argued that the adoption of LIFO results in an understatement of both assets and net income and threatens the integrity of the financial statements.[51]

Another income-distorting device is what Kohler calls "substantial-depreciation-now-and-little-depreciation-later" methods.[52] Any means of adjusting depreciation charges to base cost expirations on current value is unacceptable. Higher profits during periods of inflation, far from being illusory as some have claimed, are, he said, quite real and are represented by real increases in cash.[53] Any attempt to adjust profit figures through increases in the provision for depreciation is evidence that the accountant or businessman does not understand the real meaning of depreciation: depreciation expense is no more than the allocation of a past cost. Kohler rejected the argument that increased depreciation charges result in an income figure which more nearly reflects the earning power of the firm. He countered that investors want to know how their invested funds are being handled. They can only be misled by value-related adjustments. They are more concerned, he contended, with investment security than with earning power. Earning power is, at any rate, such a nebulous concept as to provide a basis for, at best, confusion, and, at worst, manipulative practices.

Preferable to accelerated depreciation is an appropriation of retained earnings to reflect increased replacement cost. However, a better approach is that of refreshing honesty: management can simply inform the stockholders that earned surplus and working capital necessary for replacement of fixed assets are being retained.[54]

Kohler was convinced that both LIFO and accelerated depreciation methods result from the search for devices which have as their only purpose the reduction of income taxes.[55] Tax saving does not provide an appropriate basis for accounting. Accounting can be justifiably based only on the "logical flow of controlled transactions through an enterprise."[56]

A related difficulty is the provision for deferred taxes when income determination for tax purposes differs from its determination for other reporting purposes. Kohler contended that the liability, if it exists, is too remote and too uncertain in amount and character to be accrued in current reports; and the accrual is likely to be continually replaced by similar accruals on assets not yet purchased. Therefore, no payment of these amounts will ever be made. At any rate, the liability is too indefinite to merit such recognition.

He also criticized the application of index numbers as

a means of making the income statement reflect the firm's earning power. The purpose of income measurement is to provide a retrospective, associating historical costs with related revenues. To adjust these numbers by the application of some average-related index having no real application to the conditions attaching to a particular business serves no useful purpose.[57] Furthermore, he found references to earning power so nebulous as to be without definition. The better approach is to provide a historical summary of the firm's experience, recognizing that the reader must supplement any conclusions drawn therefrom with facts which cannot possibly be reflected in the accounts.[58]

The income statement must provide a historical summary. It best accomplishes this purpose when it is based on an all-inclusive concept of income. Kohler looked to an income statement with a special section for extraordinary charges and a single income figure at the end. Such an approach has several advantages:

(1)   It is the simplest of the various suggestions thus far made.

(2)   It is easy to understand. A subtotal on the income statement before deducting the "extraordinary" items provides the figure, if such a figure is deemed necessary, for net income.

(3)   The single net income figure at the end of the inclusive income statement involves no compromise with previous representations of assets, surplus, and earnings, by the management and its auditors, to stockholders.

(4)   A consistent point of view is developed that the income statement reflects all income, expense, and losses

resulting from the year's transactions, including in "transactions" losses and other recognized expirations of cost.

(5)   It avoids the possibility of a manipulatory device which can be employed by less scrupulous business management on the marginal members of the accounting profession; and it thereby will <u>strengthen the prestige</u> of the profession.[59]

Distortions in income presentation result not from including all charges in the current statement but from relieving the current period of certain items by permitting charges to surplus or the creation and manipulation of reserves. The statements should present an objective picture which includes disclosure of the primary historical variables and the need for asset replacement.

Capital and surplus

Propositions fourteen through twenty of the Tentative Statement are designed to provide a clear distinction between paid-in capital and earned surplus, thus segregating corporate income and profits from other changes in stockholders' equity. They define those amounts to be classified in each category, condemn the use of paid-in surplus or surplus reserves to absorb losses, and require the dating of earned surplus following a corporate reorganization and the reporting of changes in capital and surplus.

<u>Two distinct elements</u>.   Eric   Kohler   was   certainly well-qualified to help the Executive Committee write the

seven surplus-related propositions of the Tentative Statement. His work on the Committee on the Definition of Earned Surplus, chaired by Arthur Andersen, led him to a thorough exploration of surplus accounts, and treatment of surplus continued to be one of his prime concerns in the development of uniform procedures.

Kohler recognized two distinct elements of net worth: paid-in capital and earned surplus. Paid-in capital represents stockholders' contributions whether they be in the form of assessments or donations. It is also the repository for proceeds from treasury stock transactions and amounts transferred from earned surplus in the event of a stock dividend or recapitalization. Earned surplus includes those amounts which represent accumulated net income less distributions to stockholders, the portion of the cost of reacquired shares which exceeds paid-in capital relating thereto, and transfers to paid-in capital due to stock dividends and recapitalizations. This position parallels that expressed by the Tentative Statement.

Surplus reserves. Kohler considered surplus reserves unnecessary. Instead, he recommended the presentation of a single earned surplus figure accompanied by a simple statement to the effect that amounts have been reserved for specified purposes.[60]

Charges to surplus. Each income statement is a chapter in a historical summary of the operations of the enterprise. Charges to surplus are thus prohibited. Each income statement purports to present fairly the results of operations for the preceding year. Subsequent recognition of charges deemed applicable to that year compromises the integrity of the previously issued financial statements.[61] As discussed in the preceding section, Kohler's primary complaint was that the dividing line between charges to income and charges to surplus had not been well drawn. Furthermore, the accountant cannot claim omniscience and therefore is ill equipped to decide what constitutes a distortion.

Reductions of earned surplus should be limited to distributions to stockholders. Enhancements are restricted to those resulting from the excess of revenues over expenses.[62] Kohler envisioned a day when these arguments would be accepted and surplus charges would be a thing of the past.

Charges to paid-in surplus are also disapproved. They may be made only if three conditions prevail: (1) stockholders give their consent; (2) such charges are limited to earned surplus deficits; and (3) write-offs to paid-in surplus are designated as recapitalizations.[63]

In the treatment of capital and surplus accounts, as well as in the measurement of income and in valuation standards, Kohler's views are in tune with those of the AAA Executive Committee. It comes as no surprise, then, that he referred often in later writings to the Association's Tentative Statement and to the events surrounding its publication.

Response to the Tentative Statement

The AAA Executive Committee attempted to establish conceptually sound positions from which the accounting profession could derive more uniform practices. The Tentative Statement was an important first step, but response was mixed. Carman Blough approved the effort, calling it "a real contribution to the accounting profession," a document whose significance and authority were enhanced by the fact that it resulted from the work of men prominent in the field. He asked the Association to continue to lead the way in the expression of sound accounting principles.[64] The practicing arm of the profession, however, largely ignored the effort. The AAA tried to encourage response, offering a life membership for the best analysis of the propositions embodied in the Tentative Statement and devoting its 1936 and 1937 meetings to the presentation of papers about the Statement. Blough's comment, above, was a part of one of those papers.

C. Rufus Rorem, one of the other speakers, applauded the AAA document as a "step in the progress of accounting as a science," a step in the direction of clarity and directness which would attempt to "tear the veil from accounting valuation and the preparation of corporate statements."[65] However, he felt that the Tentative Statement was but a first step, covering only three aspects of corporate accounting, and that the remaining task was a large one.

Victor Stempf disagreed. He feared that the Executive Committee's effort would put the profession in a straitjacket of rules and preferred instead the use of what Kohler called equivocal words and phrases such as "acceptable."[66] This reaction was evidently typical of practitioners. Another response in a similar vein was that of T. H. Sanders, who contended that in most areas where the AAA document differed from common practice, common practice was right. He was especially critical of the committee's restrictions on charges to surplus and argued that certain items, i.e., those not relating to the current year's operations, are properly charged to earned surplus since that is the repository of the profits and losses from previous years. He was also critical of the committee's attitude regarding operating reserves and charges to those reserves. His position was that setting up such reserves merely recognizes the realities of the business situation, providing for normal and foreseeable losses. Once again, current practice provided the yardstick for judging the merits of the statement.

If the AAA had provided a framework, it proved to be one which was not immediately embraced by the accounting profession as a whole. The "whatever is, is right" approach prevailed and was evidenced by the 1937 publication of A Statement of Accounting Principles, an AIA monograph outlining current practice. However, the AAA continued to examine and revise its effort to develop accounting principles.

Revisions and supplements

The AAA, and Eric Kohler in particular, was not content to rest on the merit of its Tentative Statement. In 1941 Kohler was named chairman of a Projects Committee appointed to revise the statement. The revision was undertaken not because it was felt that the original document needed an overhaul but because of a conviction that "basic accounting concepts should be given continuous study."[67] In fact, the feeling was that the earlier document needed only minor modifications. The 1941 revision, "Accounting Principles Underlying Corporate Financial Statements,"[68] is little different from its 1936 counterpart. Again the emphasis on historical cost, the commitment to the all-inclusive income statement, and the separation of contributed capital and earned surplus are primary.

The next revision, published in 1948, was actually begun during Eric Kohler's second term as president of the Association. Kohler had called in 1946 for a revision of the 1941 statement, but others hesitated. He demurred for a time, but he appointed a revision committee to begin to consider the next statement. "Accounting Concepts and Standards Underlying Corporate Financial Statements: 1948 Revision"[69] repeated the earlier propositions but also incorporated some changes in response to postwar conditions. Specifically, it took a position against restoring fixed asset values which had been expensed during the war years.

Later evidence of the Association's continuing effort in the development of accounting principles includes a total of thirteen supplementary statements (1950-1954 and 1964-1965)[70] and one further revision, published in 1957.[71] The final chapters to the principles development effort were A Statement of Basic Accounting Theory,[72] published in 1966, and A Statement on Accounting Theory and Theory Acceptance,[73] which appeared in 1977. Kohler was, of course, most intimately involved with the earlier principles statements, particularly the 1936 and 1941 manuscripts. In fact, the most recent publication, Theory and Theory Acceptance, appeared after his death.

The later works, too, espouse ideas with which one doubts Kohler would be in complete agreement. In fact, Kohler said that some of the revisions were not entirely to his liking.[74] One obvious example of an idea with which he would be uncomfortable is the departure from a strict historical cost position. Nevertheless, the effort to develop accounting principles, provided an impetus by

Kohler's 1934 editorial, became a continuing commitment for the AAA, the organization which Kohler felt had the most to contribute to its resolution.

SUMMARY

Kohler helped to lead the way in forging accounting principles, stressing the need for standards which would provide guidance and definition for the profession. As president in 1936 of the newly organized American Accounting Association, he drafted "A Tentative Statement of Accounting Principles Affecting Corporate Reports." The document was intended to provide a foundation for financial statement construction and interpretation and focused on three areas of major difficulty in corporate statements: costs and value, measurement of income, and capital and surplus. The twenty propositions are aimed at these problem areas and rest on one fundamental axiom: accounting is essentially a process of cost allocation.

Kohler's own message is consistent with that of the Tentative Statement: cost is the only objective basis for valuation, recognition, and ultimate reporting. The transaction is the source of cost data and provides the foundation for that information which furnishes orderly aid in the conduct of business and an account of management stewardship. Useful information regarding values other than cost may be recognized and supplied through forward accounting. However, historical cost provides the only acceptable basis for external reporting.

NOTES

[1]Eric L. Kohler, "Tendencies in Balance Sheet Construction," Accounting Review (December, 1926), p. 7.

[2]Eric L. Kohler, "Purview of the Government Accountant," The Federal Accountant (Spring, 1966), p. 10.

[3]Eric L. Kohler, "Accounting as a Management Control," Municipal Finance (August, 1948), p. 3.

[4]Eric L. Kohler, "Why Not Retain Historical Cost?" Journal of Accountancy (October, 1963), p. 36.

[5]Eric L. Kohler, "The Investor and Financial Statements," Accounting Review (September, 1932), p. 214.

[6]Eric L. Kohler, "Suggestions for Write-Downs," Accounting Review (March, 1931), p. 82.

[7]Kohler, "Why Not Retain Historical Cost?" p. 36.

[8]Eric L. Kohler, "Balance Sheet Standards," The Certified Public Accountant (December, 1931), p. 374.

[9]Kohler, "Tendencies in Balance Sheet Construction," p. 9.

[10]Kohler, "Balance Sheet Standards," p. 374.

[11]Ibid.

[12]Ibid.

[13]Gary John Previts and Barbara Dubis Merino, A History of Accounting in America (New York: John Wiley and Sons, 1979), pp. 237, 242.

[14]Eric L. Kohler, "Standards: A Dialogue," Accounting Review (December, 1935), p. 371.

[15]Carman G. Blough, "Early Development of Accounting Standards and Principles," in Eric Louis Kohler: Accounting's Man of Principles, W. W. Cooper and Yuji Ijiri, editors (Reston, Virginia: Reston Publishing Company, 1979),

pp. 31-40. See also David F. Hawkins, "The Development of Modern Financial Reporting Practices Among American Manufacturing Corporations" in Contemporary Studies in the Evolution of Accounting Thought, Michael Chatfield, editor (Belmont, California: Dickenson Publishing Company, Inc., 1968), pp. 249-252.

[16]Carman G. Blough, "The Need for Accounting Principles," Accounting Review (March, 1937), p. 30.

[17]Eric L. Kohler, "Accounting Principles Underlying Corporate Financial Statements: A Symposium," Foreword, Accounting Review (January, 1942), p. 1.

[18]Eric L. Kohler, "Research Problems," Accounting Review (March, 1931), p. 81.

[19]Kohler, "Standards: A Dialogue," pp. 370-379.

[20]John L. Carey, "The CPA's Professional Heritage, Part IV," Accounting Historian's Working Papers, Volume II (Atlanta, Georgia: Academy of Accounting Historians, 1975), p. 227.

[21]Ibid.

[22]Kohler, "Standards Must Come," pp. 335-336.

[23]Howard C. Greer, "Benchmarks and Beacons," Accounting Review (January, 1956), p. 4.

[24]Eric L. Kohler, "In All My Years," The Accounting Historian (Spring, 1975), p. 4.

[25]"A Statement of Objectives of the American Accounting Association," Accounting Review (March, 1936), p. 1.

[26]Kohler, "In All My Years," p. 4.

[27]"A Statement of Objectives of the AAA," p. 2.

[28]"A Tentative Statement of Accounting Principles Affecting Corporate Reports," Accounting Review (June, 1936), p. 187.

[29]Ibid., p. 188.

[30]Howard C. Greer, "What Are Accepted Principles of Accounting?" Accounting Review (March, 1938), p. 30.

[31]"A Statement of Objectives of the AAA," p. 3.

[32]Stephen A. Zeff, editor, The American Accounting Association: Its First Fifty Years (Evanston, Illinois: American Accounting Association, 1966), p. 44.

[33]Kohler, "Why Not Retain Historical Cost?" p. 36.

[34]Ibid., p. 36.

[35]Ibid., p. 39.

[36]Ibid., p. 38.

[37]Eric L. Kohler, Review of The Elusive Art of Accounting, Journal of Accountancy (August, 1966), p. 88.

[38]Eric L. Kohler, "Restoration of Fixed Asset Values to the Balance Sheet: First Negative," Accounting Review (April, 1947), pp. 202-203.

[39]Eric L. Kohler, "How Much Depreciation," Illinois Society of CPAs Bulletin (December, 1947), p. 9.

[40]Kohler, "Why Not Retain Historical Cost?" p. 40.

[41]Kohler, "How Much Depreciation," p. 5.

[42]Kohler, "Why Not Retain Historical Cost?" p. 39.

[43]Ibid., pp. 40-41.

[44]Ibid.

[45]Eric L. Kohler, "Some Tentative Propositions Underlying Consolidated Reports," Accounting Review (March, 1938), p. 67.

[46]Eric L. Kohler, "Surplus," Contemporary Accounting (American Institute of Accountants, 1945), p. 2.

[47]Ibid.

[48]Eric L. Kohler, "Suggestions for Write-Downs," Accounting Review (March, 1931), p. 82.

[49]Eric L. Kohler, "Changing Concepts of Business Income," Ohio Certified Public Accountant (Summer, 1952), p. 7.

[50]Eric L. Kohler, "Background for Management-Accounting Techniques," N.A.A. Bulletin (October, 1961), p. 12.

[51] Ibid.

[52] Ibid.

[53] Kohler, "How Much Depreciation," p. 8.

[54] Eric L. Kohler, "Depreciation and the Price Level: Third Negative," Accounting Review (April, 1948), p. 136.

[55] Eric L. Kohler, "Research Potentials in International Accounting," Proceedings of the International Conference on Accounting Education, 1952, p. 90.

[56] Kohler, "Background for Management Accounting Techniques," p. 13.

[57] Kohler, "Depreciation and the Price Level: Third Negative," p. 136.

[58] Ibid.

[59] Kohler, "Surplus," p. 5.

[60] Ibid., p. 10.

[61] Ibid., p. 4.

[62] Ibid., p. 2.

[63] Eric L. Kohler, "Dated Surplus," Accounting Review (September, 1934), p. 257.

[64] Blough, "Need for Accounting Principles," p. 30.

[65] C. Rufus Rorem, "Accounting Theory: A Critique of the Tentative Statement of Accounting Principles," Accounting Review (June, 1937), p. 138.

[66] Victor H. Stempf, "A Critique of the Tentative Statement of Accounting Principles," Accounting Review (March, 1938), p. 56.

[67] Zeff, p. 50.

[68] American Accounting Association, "Accounting Principles Underlying Corporate Financial Statements," Accounting Review (June, 1941), pp. 133-139.

[69] American Accounting Association, "Accounting Concepts and Standards Underlying Corporate Financial Statements: 1948 Revision," Accounting Review (October, 1948), pp. 339-344.

[70]
1. Reserves and Retained Income (1950)
2. Price Level Changes and Financial Statements (1951)
3. Current Assets and Current Liabilities (1951)
4. Accounting Principles and Taxable Income (1952)
5. Accounting Corrections (1953)
6. Inventory Pricing and Changes in Price Levels (1953)
7. Consolidated Financial Statements (1954)
8. Standards of Disclosure for Published Financial Reports (1954)

The remaining supplements deal with long-lived assets, inventories, realization, entity, and matching.

[71]"Accounting and Reporting Standards for Corporate Financial Statements: 1957 Revision," Accounting Review (October, 1957), pp. 536-546.

[72]American Accounting Association, A Statement of Basic Accounting Theory (Evanston, Illinois: AAA, 1966).

[73]American Accounting Association, A Statement on Accounting Theory and Theory Acceptance (Sarasota, Florida: AAA, 1977).

[74]Eric L. Kohler, Tennessee Valley Authority Oral History (Memphis, Tennessee: Memphis State University Oral History Research Office, February, 1971), Interview #1, p. 7.

V

ARBITER OF DEFINITIONS

The writing for which Eric Kohler is perhaps best known and that to which he devoted much of his energy is, of course, the Dictionary for Accountants. Published in five editions during his lifetime, the work has been described as his "springboard for expounding his philosophy of accounting that has been molded over the years by his experience."[1] This chapter contains an examination of Kohler's lifelong interest in accounting language beginning with his early service on the terminology committees and continuing through the years when the dictionary became an individual project, an expression of his accounting philosophy. It provides an examination of the need for definitions, as Kohler saw it, and the criteria which those definitions must meet. Finally, aspects of selected definitions are presented in order to identify the dictionary as not merely a reference work but as a personal treatise.

THE TERMINOLOGY COMMITTEES

The seed for the dictionary was sown during the years 1929 to 1931 when Kohler worked with Arthur Andersen on the American Institute's Committee on the Definition of Earned Surplus. His subsequent tenure on the Committee on Terminology, first as secretary under Robert Montgomery's chairmanship and later as chairman himself, reinforced his interest in laying a foundation for more precise communication. He later recalled the committee's efforts and their reception by the Institute:

> We immediately began collecting and sifting suggested definitions from a broad assortment of individuals and firms. In the summer of 1936 . . . I did indeed cloister myself in a sixth-floor room of an east-side rooming house for two weeks, and prepared an initial draft of a report (to the audible chorus of termites busily consuming one of the doorway panels). Our committee then spent two days together making final changes, and on August 1, 1936, we put out 200 numbered copies of a 105-page mimeographed "Preliminary Report" containing about 1000 terms . . . . The AIA Council did not even acknowledge receipt of the report, GOM coming out with a statement that under our system of free enterprise accountants were free to devise their own definitions. . . . The following year the Committee was dropped, the general conclusion being that GOM might be right.[2]

But Kohler, convinced as he was that definition is essential to the development of sound theory, could not let the work end there, and the dictionary became an individual effort.

AN INDIVIDUAL PROJECT

When the Committee was abolished, Montgomery encouraged Kohler to continue on his own. Although other responsibilities delayed Kohler's work, his effort to extract essences from the accountant's language had begun.

In the years between the dictionary's conception in 1937 and its ultimate publication in 1952, he rejoined Arthur Andersen & Co., edited the Accounting Review, served as controller of the Tennessee Valley Authority and later the Economic Cooperation Administration, and served the War Production Board as a management consultant. Finally, in 1950 he was approached by Prentice-Hall about preparing the 1934 report for publication. With the help of a number of individuals, and especially William W. Cooper, the work took shape. New terms were added; definitions for other terms were broadened, recast, and revised until the dictionary became not only a reference work for the profession but also Kohler's personal contribution to the development of accounting principles.

A Tentative Effort

He considered the first edition tentative, an effort to solicit comments and suggestions for revision. A 1951 letter to F. Sewell Bray makes this intention clear:

> . . . the publishers . . . have agreed to put out a preliminary edition which will be announced shortly and given as wide a circulation as possible in an

effort to elicit more criticisms than I have been able to gather in recent months, and later--say within two years--to put out a more complete and wholly revised edition.[3]

In fact, the original idea was to put out a new edition every two years. Although that particular goal was not met, the revision process was a constant one.

A Continuing Task

The dictionary was a work to whose revision and refinement its author was devoted. He received and responded to letters from accounting professionals from all parts of the world. These letters offered new terms and definitions and questioned existing ones. In addition, Kohler sought input from those who might best be able to evaluate his definitions. For example, in 1973 he asked Elmer Staats, U.S. Comptroller General, to comment on and revise as necessary the definition of Comptroller General.[4] And when he heard Marshall Armstrong use the term "thrust of accounting" at an AICPA meeting, he tried his hand at a definition and submitted it to Armstrong for his reaction.[5]

Whether responding to suggestions or constructing definitions of new terms, Kohler was absorbed in the dictionary's development. One colleague testifies:

> Kohler quickly threw himself into each idea and, not being easily satisfied with modes of expression by others, he would re-write and rewrite each such contribution until it fitted into the grander scheme of things that he was visualizing for his dictionary.[6]

The task was one to which he was truly dedicated. He told another associate:

> Getting out a work of this kind keeps on being an exciting business for me. There is never enough time for it and after a couple of months on other things there will be scarcely a page that to me, anyway, will not demand some minor or even major overhauling.[7]

As the field of accounting broadened and other professionals offered suggestions, the dictionary was revised. Thus, Kohler's "adventure in lexicography"[8] grew from 2,275 to more than 3,000 entries during the twenty-three years of its passage from first to fifth editions, encompassing, for example, new mathematical/statistical or governmental terms as the profession expanded.[9]

THE NEED FOR DEFINITIONS

Kohler recognized early the need for definitions as a starting point for the sound development of accounting. Perhaps this recognition was partially due to the influence of Arthur Andersen who, Kohler recalls, began in the early 1920s to call for attempts to form standard, agreed-upon definitions.[10] By 1926 Kohler had himself taken up the cry. In "Tendencies in Balance Sheet Construction," he criticized the profession for having taken to the use of equivocal English, accusing accountants of using language interpretable only to themselves and chosen less to facilitate communication than to provide protection.[11] He was convinced that terminological standards were an essential prerequisite to financial statements which would be truly useful. For example, in a review of a Canadian terminological publication, he said:

> The language of accountants, consisting in large measure of combinations of borrowed words, is sorely wanting in neatness, precision, and resistance to change; in fact, it openly invites the confusion of the whole with its parts, and of the symbol with the image the term is expected to invoke.[12]

His complaint that "accountancy lacks definitions"[13] continued to underlie much of his writing.

Definitions and Standards

Balance sheet standards are inextricably tied to the use of standard terminology. As evidence of this connection, witness the report of the 1929 Committee on Technical Affairs, which Kohler chaired. Its first recommendation for the development of accounting standards was the creation of a body of definitions. This is the essential starting point. The relationship between definitions and standards is a straightforward one:

> Definitions are standards; but standards embrace also the axioms and the particular variety of reasoning through which our performances must clear. There does not appear to be much difference between an axiom and a definition, especially in accounting, except that for the definition we substitute a single word or phrase. Both are assumptions. Both are starting points. Both provide us with working tools for the construction of theories, logical processes, and conclusions. . . .[14]

In order that logical principles may be developed, it is necessary first to have achieved a careful formulation of concepts.

Criteria for Definitions

The purpose of a definition is to make communication possible by specifying the qualities of <u>universals</u>. A universal is the "essence of any logical genus or species."[15] Kohler, in fact, described his dictionary as an exercise in extracting essences.[16] It is in this quest for universals that he established criteria necessary for definitions. They are:

(1) It must set forth the fundamental and unique attribute or attributes of all members of the class but of no other class.

(2) It may be stated in terms of the next larger class, thus avoiding a more elaborate differentia.

(3) If the class and the differences of a term cannot readily be recounted, a <u>genetic</u> definition may be resorted to; that is, the sense of a thing may be gained from a knowledge of how it is produced.

(4) There must be no <u>circulus in definiendo</u>, or repetition of the term to be defined.

(5) Where the same meaning attaches to more than one word or term, preference should be given to one of them.

(6) Where a word has more than one meaning, the separate uses must be appropriately distinguished.

(7) Plain, direct language is highly desirable.

(8) A negative statement must not be used except where the positive has a clear disadvantage.[17]

Definitions which meet these criteria will provide a foundation for more effective communication.

THE ACCOUNTING MYSTIQUE

Vague Terms

Kohler was especially critical of loose terms whose meanings were kept sufficiently vague to suit a variety of speakers, listeners, and situations. At one point he accused the accounting profession of having relied on several "esoteric terms whose definitions have been studiously avoided" and which have, as a consequence, "acquired a mystique that has imprisoned their users in a conceptual world only incidentally related to the mundane realities that confront accounting and accountants."[18] The use of such terms was not, he was convinced, accidental. It resulted directly from a desire to be on the safe side. As a result, one finds in the accountant's vocabulary a "generous supply of clichés, slogans, and other familiar phrases for an undiscriminating and seemingly never-ceasing application to a great variety of situations."[19] Examples of this professional malaise are readily found, Kohler was quick to point out, in official pronouncements or an auditor's average long-form report.

Among the terms which Kohler especially singled out for criticism are certain descriptive adjectives. Some of those deplorable attributives are: <u>acceptable</u>, <u>adequate</u>, <u>advantageous</u>, <u>appropriate</u>, <u>desirable</u>, <u>material</u>, <u>meaningful</u>, <u>permissible</u>, <u>practicable</u>, <u>preferable</u>, <u>proper</u>, <u>rational</u>, <u>realistic</u>, <u>reasonable</u>, <u>significant</u>, <u>sound</u>, <u>systematic</u>, <u>useful</u>, <u>fair</u>, and <u>logical</u>. The use of such adjectives in official publications he found to be, at the least, excessive, and the object of their use he found deplorable: as he saw it, the idea was to employ words which were sufficiently vague and interchangeable so that two individuals--indeed an entire committee such as the Committee on Accounting Procedure--may reach agreement or at least avoid making any statement specific enough to engender disagreement. He specifically cited one Institute bulletin in which such adjectives appeared no fewer than fifty-seven times.[20] His conclusion was:

> The moral of all this for those of you whose mother tongue is not English is that, in your reading of our official pronouncements you need neither pause nor to translate when encountering any of our interchangeable adjectives. If no meanings then emerge, it may be that none was intended.[21]

The words were deliberately chosen to convey no real meaning but merely to provide a hedge against taking a firm position.

On another occasion, Kohler explained at some length the development of accountancy's stopgap terms:

In some instances they conferred authority on dicta for which no logical foundation had as yet been established. This was inevitable in situations where matters of immediate concern to the profession had to be treated authoritatively but without any buildup of historical background. In other instances there may have been differences among those whose ideas were combined in a single statement, and an ostensibly harmless word or phrase was chosen as a substitute for a long (and possibly what was feared would be regarded as an irrelevant) discussion of side issues. Moreover, experience has taught us that a group of individuals can more often agree on a conclusion than on the reasons contributing to it. Again, in numerous situations the compilers seemed to fear the effects of enunciating rules that would be inflexible--where, for example, exceptions, already well established or perhaps yet to arise, might also require at least tacit indorsement; those whose stopgap characteristics had already gained some recognition within the profession, were therefore in order. Finally, the urge for uniformity as a defense against irresponsible charges of impropriety has led to the common employment of certain words as a protective device--the idea being, as I am sure most of us believe, that in unity there is strength.[22]

Again Kohler's complaint was that terms were chosen not to communicate but to obfuscate.

The American Institute, of course, bore the brunt of the criticism. The principles statements of the AAA Kohler found "exceptionally free from such words and phrases."[23] In the AIA publications, however, he found an abundance of these unfortunate terms. He pointed out and even listed the number of times such slippery, interchangeable words were used in AIA bulletins.[24] And he quoted one particularly guilty sentence: "The employment of sound, practicable principles in significant situations is an earmark of the acceptable

accountant of today."[25]   The only possible improvement, he
suggested, would be:

> Permissible applications of accounting that are
> sound and proper, appropriate and significant, and
> both practicable and useful, seem not only to be
> acceptable and adequate, but also to be reasonable
> and desirable, even preferable.[26]

Such a statement, he contended, is meaningless.

The Auditor's Report

The auditor's report Kohler saw as a prime example that
language can be used to mystify rather than to clarify. He
referred to the phraseology "We hereby certify, in our
opinion" as "absurd grotesquery inherited from those earlier
generations of accountants who spoke in terms intended to
keep the world adequately mystified."[27] Why not simply say
"We believe," he asked. In fact, he contended that the
overall wording of the audit report was evidence of awkward
phrasing containing little or no meaning. This condition was
not surprising since the goal, as he saw it, had been not to
convey information to the reader but to protect the
accountant.

Kohler's suggestion was that auditors should establish
certain minimum requirements for audits and should then
indicate that these requirements have been met by attaching
to the financial statements a simple "approved by" followed
by the name of the firm. If the report must be qualified,
the appropriate certification would read "approved, with the

following qualifications." Simple, unequivocal language was the goal. This approach, he believed, met the demands of good practice and bound the accountant to the exercise of caution and good judgment.[28]

A PERSONAL CRUSADE

Other Terminology Projects

Kohler's concern for a common language for accountants led him to involve himself in terminology projects other than his own. For example, regarding the Cost Accounting Standards Board's terminology project, he wrote to Elmer Staats suggesting that it was highly desirable to avoid conflicts among groups compiling definitions and expressing his belief that without a common language, useful standards could not be developed.[29]

Making the Dictionary Accessible

Its author closely supervised every detail of the dictionary's production and fought hard to make the volume accessible to a wider number of people. His correspondence with the publisher testifies to his insistence on being consulted about page and type sizes as well as production schedules.[30] He battled for a paperback fifth edition, the idea being that it would be easier to handle and less expensive and would therefore be more useful to more people. At one point he explained:

> The DICTIONARY is not a textbook although like any dictionary, it includes among its aims helpfulness to students. Its main "thrust" is to bring together--as completely as possible at this somewhat critical time--the float of terms currently in use by the profession of which teachers are but a fraction. . . . From all this, a broader distribution, encouraged by a shrink in size (notwithstanding increased content), and smaller weight and price, has appeared to be most desirable. . . . My intention has been to make it portable, cheaper, and more suitable for desk and briefcase than shelf, thus serving other than dictionary purposes.[31]

He was finally forced to give up the fight but refused to do so gracefully, persisting in his belief that the book should be lower in price, easier to handle, and more readily available to students, to persons abroad, and to those in related fields.[32]

SOME DEFINITIONS

Accountancy, according to Kohler, grew in a rather haphazard fashion and neither had nor took the time to develop an underlying philosophy. The Kohler dictionary was intended as an effort in the development of such a philosophy. In the preface to the dictionary's sixth--and first posthumous--edition, its editors testify to the role of the dictionary as more than a reference work:

> For one thing he saw this work as a part of a continuing effort for developing a general set of accounting principles and for improving (in every sense of the word) accounting practice. For another thing he saw it as an opportunity to reach beyond accounting to bring in terms and concepts from related disciplines and to adjust or adapt them for use in accounting. The result was much

more than a dictionary, or at least it was much more than a dictionary of accounting. At numerous points--and especially with words that he regarded as basic to accounting--Kohler filled out the definitions with brief essays and elaborations that are really gems of synoptic insight into accounting issues, problems and practices at very basic levels.[33]

Some indication of Kohler's intention in constructing the dictionary may be gained by examining a few of these definitions. The following section is devoted to exploring some of the dictionary's basic concepts, including the philosophical building blocks, or primitives, and the definitions of some terms with which Kohler was especially concerned.

Principles, Postulates, Propositions

Kohler's exploration into basic concepts and their relationship to the development of accounting theory began with an examination of what he called primitives. These he defined as "foundation or linkage terms . . . essential to building accounting concepts that could be defined by the employment of language common to other disciplines."[34] These primitives are the building blocks of accounting theory. There are 178 such terms, including assumption, convention, proposition, postulate, and principle.

A basic building block is the axiom. It is "a general statement, the truth of which is not questioned."[35] Axioms in accounting include the following:

(a)   An economic unit has an identity apart from other
      economic units

(b)   The life of a typical economic unit extends
      indefinitely into the future

(c)   Relations between economic units are carried on by
      means of identifiable, separable and measurable
      transactions

(d)   The transactions of an economic unit are expressed
      in terms of a common medium of exchange

(e)   Transactions collectively measure both economic
      wealth and economic activity.[36]

Postulate is synonomous with axiom; an assumption, likewise,
is a starting point for a line of thought or action. A
convention, unlike an axiom, is a practice observed by common
consent even though it is recognized that other practices,
equally defensible, are available. Placing debits on the
left and credits on the right is an example. Once chosen, a
convention becomes valuable because it facilitates
communication.

From axioms, postulates, and conventions, principles
are built. Principle may be used synonymously with standard,
but it is more appropriately a term of broader application.
A standard is a normative principle; it generally falls short
of the ideal but is accepted in an effort to promote
uniformity.

A proposition is any declarative statement. A rule, in
contrast to a principle, "covers a narrower field of activity
and allows less discretion in its application."[37]   A

principle, on the other hand, provides the best possible guide to choice among alternatives. Accounting principles are propositions accepted within the profession which serve as an explanation of practice and an aid in selecting courses of action. As such, they should be simple and clear guides to professional development.

From these building blocks, Kohler's accounting theory is constructed. Based upon the axioms described above, his conviction that the transaction is primary emerges. Other primary concerns, particularly the emphasis on historical cost, are logical extensions of this position. The purpose of accounting is to record, classify, and report on transactions. The emphasis on reporting and recording transactions mandates complete information and prohibits charges to surplus or other potentially manipulative devices. It is here that Kohler's definitional foundation for principles and his personal high principles intermingle. And his positions, as explored in Chapter Two, are evident in the dictionary.

The discussion of accounting principles provides one example. He complained that the AICPA had failed to provide a consistent framework; nor had the Institute's standards generally pointed to universally applicable principles. He did, however, identify certain generalizations emerging from the pronouncements of professional bodies, generalizations which most would classify as principles. These may be summarized as follows:

1. The objective of accounting is classifying, recording, summarizing, and reporting transactions.

2. Much of accounting is designed to aid management in achieving the lowest possible cost.

3. Asset valuation is based on price, determined in an arms-length transaction.

4. The excess of price over the book value of a group of assets is considered excess earning power and is amortized over the years to which it is imputed.

5. Transfers of assets between commonly controlled entities should be priced at the seller's depreciated cost.

6. Cost provides the only objective basis for valuation. Because it is based on actual transactions, it is the most useful basis for management, investor, and consumer.

7. Valuation reflecting appreciation or the application of index numbers is an inappropriate basis for accounting records or reports. It may, however, be furnished as supplementary information.

8. Forms of accretion are recognized only when realized through the sale of the asset.

9. Straight-line depreciation provides the simplest and most nearly accurate means of allocating the cost of a limited-life asset.

10. Inventory should be carried at an amount not exceeding its cost, market value, or net realizable value, whichever is lower. While LIFO inventory valuation provides a tax advantage, it remains a violation of logical inventory flow assumptions.

11. Bond discount is properly offset against the face value of the indebtedness; however, it is in practice frequently classified as a deferred charge.

12. Unamortized discount is an expense of the year of refunding.

13. Income from long-term construction contracts may be recognized in proportion to billings made or collections received. However, gross profit related to installment sales is generally recognized at the time of sale.

14. A breakdown of sales or cost of sales by product or department may be necessary for statement users, as may comparative data.

15. Revenue and expenses recognized during the accounting period, even though associated with past periods, are to be included in the income statement.

16. A separate section of the income statement identifies revenue and expenses not attributable to operations of the current period. This section includes such items as extraordinary and nonrecurring gains and losses.

17. Provisions for contingencies do not belong in the income statement but are reservations of retained earnings.

18. Stockholders equity includes paid-in capital and retained earnings.

19. When a corporation reacquires shares of its own stock, paid-in capital is charged with the average amount paid for the stock. Amounts exceeding this average are charged to retained earnings. Resales are treated as original issues.

20. A reduction of par or stated value is a quasi-reorganization and requires stockholder approval and subsequent dating of retained earnings.[38]

While at least some of these principles may indeed be, as Kohler claimed, propositions generally endorsed by the profession as a whole, they are undoubtedly also propositions which may be identified with the author's own accounting philosophy. As such, they constitute evidence of the subjectivity of the dictionary.

Fairness

One of the clearest evidences of the interrelationship of Eric Kohler's dedication to the development of accounting principles and his dedication to the development of accounting terminology is found in his exploration of the concept of fairness. In 1959 he had heard George O. May express his conviction that there should be only one guiding principle of accounting: fairness. Kohler explored this idea in his dictionary, revising in the fourth edition the definition put forward in the first three.

The earlier definition had associated fairness with the concepts of truth, justness, equity, and candor in financial statement presentation. The revised one spelled out in considerably more detail the criteria which must be considered (see Exhibit I). In order for the comprehensive, twenty-five part definition of fairness to be met, certain conditions must attach to the auditor's examination, to client accounting methods and controls, to the financial statements, and to disclosure of departures from the established conditions. Fairness is, acccording to this definition, a broad-based concept having as its touchstone the perception not of the accountant nor of management but of the financial statement user. Kohler would concede that fairness is a guiding principle of accounting, but he doubted that it could be called the one guiding principle. He viewed fairness not as a substitute for principle but as a recognition of the need for minimum reporting standards.[39] He insisted that those conditions necessary to fair presentation be given concrete expression.

Fixed Asset Valuation

Kohler's definition of fixed asset[40] includes a lengthy essay detailing the objections to valuing fixed assets at amounts in excess of cost. These include (1) Profits arise

EXHIBIT I*

Conditions Which Have Been Met in an Unqualified
Short-Form Report

The phrase "present fairly" in the public
accountant's unmodified short-form report means
that no less than the following conditions have
been met:

As to the auditor's examination

1. His independence, reflected in the conduct of
   his audit and affirmed by the character of his
   report, is unquestioned.
2. No limitation, natural or imposed by the
   client, has reduced the scope of his audit
   below the level he considers minimal.
3. Records and other supporting evidence required
   by him have been available to and utilized by
   him.
4. He has tested receivables by correspondence and
   substantiated opening and closing inventories
   by observation, or he has satisfied himself
   with respect to these items by other means of
   his choice.
5. He has accepted responsibility for the report
   of another auditor (e.g., on a branch or
   subsidiary) which has been combined or
   consolidated in the financial statements
   accompanying his report, or he has submitted
   the other's report collaterally with his own.
6. Contingencies and other uncertainties affecting
   present and future interpretations of
   financial statements have been evaluated by
   him and reported as he judges necessary.

---

*From: Eric L. Kohler, "Fairness," Journal of
Accountancy (December, 1967), p. 59. Copyright (c)
1967 by the American Institute of Certified Public
Accountants, Inc. Opinions expressed in the
Journal of Accountancy are those of its editors and
contributors. Publication in the Journal of
Accountancy does not constitute endorsement by the
AICPA or its committees.

7. His short-form-report language follows the current professional standard, on occasion modified by him to express a qualified, adverse, or disclaimer of opinion; or he prepares no report and dissociates himself from the financial statements he has examined.
8. In general, he has exercised professional care and judgment throughout his examination.

As to the client's internal controls and accounting methods

9. Internal controls have been adequate.
10. Accounting principles have been observed and the client's applied accounting policies and procedures have been acceptable.
11. Accounting policies and applications have been consistent throughout the audit period and the period preceding.
12. The books of account have been brought into agreement with the financial statements.

As to the financial statements and appended notes

13. Terminology common to financial statements is employed or notes defining unfamiliar terms are provided.
14. The arrangement of financial statement items follows the conventional pattern.
15. The financial statements are comparable in form and item with those of similar organizations.
16. Unexpired acquisition cost is the basis of asset valuation; any other basis is described and the amount by which it differs from acquisition cost less accumulated depreciation acquistion cost appears.
17. Depreciation methods for both accounting and tax purposes, and current provisions and accumulations, are revealed.
18. More-than-minor differences between net income and taxable income are explained.
19. Annual rentals, and other provisions of general interest in long-term leases, pension plans, compensation agreements, and stock-option and bonus plans are set forth.

20. An unusual large-scale transaction, an important change in activities, or other major post-balance-sheet event or condition is disclosed.

21. No misstatement or misrepresentation known to the auditor is reflected in the financial statements.

22. Facts and conditions are included without which the financial statements might be interpreted as misleading.

23. Information that may contribute to the reader's better understanding is provided, even though without it the statements cannot technically be regarded as misleading.

24. Financial statements and their attached notes are management's although prepared by the auditor, or added to or modified at his instance; any item omitted from them judged by the auditor to be of importance appears in his report.

As to any departure, deemed by the auditor to be material in character or amount, from any of the preceding conditions

25. His report identifies the item with the accompanying financial statements (and attached notes) and provides information designed to aid an outsider's appraisal of its significance

from sales, and to record earnings before the earning process has actually taken place is artificial and uninformative; (2) Established earning ability, not increased value resulting from appraisals, influences investors; (3) Appraisal values may well be based on unrealistic assumptions; (4) The notion of "true economic cost" confuses future costs with present ones and fails to recognize the realities of a competitive marketplace where the producer who has older, lower fixed-asset costs truly has a competitive edge.

Also included is a lengthy discussion of internal controls over fixed assets. This section is introduced by the complaint that such controls have often been inadequate, a complaint that is also evident in other of Kohler's writings. Again, these positions mirror those which he had expressed elsewhere.

Net Income

The definition of net income[41] addresses the differences among professionals regarding the items which are appropriately included in periodic net income. The author's own preference may be inferred from the fact that he gives the arguments for the current operating performance approach approximately one-sixth the coverage that he gives the all-inclusive approach.

The current operating performance statement is supported by three arguments which may be reduced to the single proposition that the income statement should reflect regular, recurring (or typical) items. For the all-inclusive concept of net income, Kohler presents nine supporting reasons, which may be summarized as follows: The income statement reports on events and on management decisions. To exclude some events or decisions is to distort the picture and invite manipulation; and because there are no well-defined criteria for deciding which items will be excluded, those decisions may not be consistently made. Only by including all items of revenue and expense, gain and loss can the statement user be assured an objective, informative report which becomes part of the story of operating results of the entity over the years. Providing disclosure regarding the nonroutine nature of certain items and segregating unusual or nonrecurring items from operating income satisfies the need for identifying separately those items not attributable to the regular, recurring activities of the enterprise. These arguments are the basis for Kohler's belief that the income statement should provide a historical summary.

Activity Accounting

The dictionary's definition of <u>activity accounting</u>[42] is indeed an essay on the principal features and uses of an activity accounting system. This concept, which Kohler strongly advocated over the years for both governmental and private sector entities, is discussed fully in chapter six. At the present time it is important to note only that the definition of activity accounting which is contained in the dictionary provides another example of Kohler's having used the book to provide insightful essays and elaboration on accounting issues. He defines the purpose and uses of an activity accounting system: to aid in conforming performance to plan by providing a mechanism for budgetary and operational controls. He then details the components of the system: projects, programs, organizational units, the activity accounts, and associated reports and responsibility. Activity accounting, like many other concepts, is not simply defined. It is explained.

Direct Costing

Another essay is provided in the definition of direct costing.[43] The technique is fully described, and its principal uses and limitations are explored. Kohler explores its usefulness in controlling costs, planning, determining periodic income and financial condition, and estimating periodic inventories.

More than a Dictionary

Many of the terms included in the dictionary are followed by what may be described as explanations rather than definitions. Balance sheet, for example, is followed by a two-page description of balance sheet format, classification, and valuation.[44] The definition of <u>asset</u> is likewise not merely definition but a full explication of the concept, accounting treatment, and valuation of assets.[45] In like manner, <u>bond discount</u> details the treatment of this item,[46] and <u>inventory valuation</u> discusses possible alternative approaches.[47] And the list continues. It comes as no surprise, then, that those who are familiar with the dictionary stress its importance as much more than a standard lexicographic work.

SUMMARY

The Kohler dictionary is indeed much more than a dictionary. It became the author's vehicle not only for providing a foundation for the development of accounting principles but also for expounding his own professional philosophy. The rewriting, recasting, and expanding became a lifelong task to which he was firmly committed. Through its five editions the work became Kohler's springboard for expressing his accounting theory. In this chapter the development of his interest in the language of accountants has been traced from the early days on the terminology committees through the dictionary's inception and development. An examination of his conviction regarding the need for definitions and their interrelationship with accounting standards has been provided. Obstructing the development of standards and emphasizing the need for definitions were certain vague terms which Kohler saw generously used in many official pronouncements. In this chapter, his criticism of the use of such terms has been examined. Finally, certain of the definitions contained in the dictionary have been reviewed in order to underline the work's importance as something more than a dictionary: within its pages Kohler has presented a collection of essays which provide insight into accounting issues and problems.

NOTES

[1]James Nolan, "It's Much More Than a Dictionary," Journal of Accountancy (May, 1972), p. 22.

[2]Letter from Eric Kohler to Stephen A. Zeff, 31 July 1971.

[3]Letter from Eric Kohler to F. Sewell Bray, 21 September 1951.

[4]Letter from Eric Kohler to Elmer Staats, 9 July 1973.

[5]Letter from Eric Kohler to Marshall Armstrong, 5 November 1973.

[6]Preface to Kohler's Dictionary for Accountants, W. W. Cooper and Yuji Ijiri, editors (Englewood Cliffs, New Jersey: Prentice-Hall, Inc., 1982). This is the sixth and first posthumous edition of the dictionary. Subsequent references to Kohler's Dictionary for Accountants will be to this edition. References to Kohler, Dictionary, will be to the fifth edition, authored by Eric Kohler, unless otherwise indicated.

[7]Letter from Eric Kohler to Lawrence Vance, 14 May 1957.

[8]Eric L. Kohler, A Dictionary for Accountants (Englewood Cliffs, New Jersey: Prentice-Hall, Inc., 1952), p. v. The 1952 publication is the dictionary's first edition. Subsequent references are to the 1975 fifth edition.

[9]The sixth edition, Kohler's Dictionary for Accountants, contains 4,539 terms.

[10]Eric L. Kohler, "In All My Years," The Accounting Historian (Spring, 1975), p. 4.

[11]Eric L. Kohler, "Language of Accounting," Journal of Accountancy (August, 1957), p. 91.

[12]Eric L. Kohler, "Earned Surplus," Accounting Review (September, 1929), p. 192.

[13]Ibid.

[14]Eric L. Kohler, "Some Principles for Terminologists," Accounting Review (American Accounting Association, March, 1935), p. 32.

[15]Ibid., p. 31.

[16]Kohler, "In All My Years," p. 4.

[17]Kohler, "Some Principles for Terminologists," p. 32.

[18]Eric L. Kohler, "On Developing International Accounting Meanings," International Journal of Accounting, Education and Research (Fall, 1965), p. 36.

[19]Ibid.

[20]Ibid., p. 38.

[21]Ibid.

[22]Eric L. Kohler, "Something About Accounting Language," Massachusetts Society of CPAs News Bulletin (October, 1954), p. 3.

[23]Ibid.

[24]Kohler's list, compiled from the 42 bulletins of the Committee on Accounting Procedure, follows:

proper	127	adequate	37
reasonable	95	permissible	30
acceptable	80	preferable	29
appropriate	78	useful	28
desirable	74	practicable	23
significant	66	sound	15

And these figures, he noted, do not include those appearances of these words in a "well-defined sense." From "Something About Accounting Language," p. 4.

[25]Ibid., p. 5.

[26]Ibid. As another example, he quoted from a systems prospectus prepared by an unidentified accounting firm: "We wish to call your attention to the desirability of permissible applications of accounting policy that over the years have proven sound and proper. These applications will be found to be both practicable and useful in your case, greatly preferable to the policy now deemed adequate by the management. A uniform, reasonable accounting policy to which a great deal of attention is now considered appropriate in enlightened financial circles, we suggest as a sound course

for you to pursue." And Kohler translates: "We may have little to offer, but we want your business." From an unpublished, untitled manuscript.

[27]Eric L. Kohler, "Modernizing Certificates," Accounting Review (September, 1931), p. 231.

[28]Eric L. Kohler, "Meaningless Certification," Accounting Review (June, 1931), p. 145.

[29]Letter from Eric Kohler to Elmer Staats, 9 July 1973.

[30]Letters from Eric Kohler to Donald Schaeffer, 4 December 1974; Shirley Covington, 7 October 1974; and Garret White, 10 January 1973 and 15 April 1974.

[31]Letter from Eric Kohler to Shirley Covington, 7 October 1974.

[32]Letter from Eric Kohler to Howard Warrington, April, 1974.

[33]From a draft of the preface to Kohler's Dictionary for Accountants, provided by William W. Cooper.

[34]Eric L. Kohler, "On Developing International Accounting Meanings," International Journal of Accounting, Education and Research (Fall, 1965), p. 39.

[35]Kohler, Dictionary, p. 50.

[36]Ibid., p. 51.

[37]Ibid., p. 413.

[38]Ibid., pp. 12-14.

[39]Kohler, "Fairness," Journal of Accountancy (December, 1967), p. 58. See also Dictionary, pp. 205-206.

[40]Kohler, Dictionary, pp. 209-216.

[41]Ibid., pp. 319-321.

[42]Ibid., pp. 20-22.

[43]Ibid., pp. 177-180.

[44]Ibid., pp. 53-55.

[45]Ibid., pp. 39-41.

[46] *Ibid.*, pp. 64-65.

[47] *Ibid.*, pp. 272-275.

VI

ACCOUNTING FOR GOVERNMENT AGENCIES

Much of Eric Kohler's professional life was devoted to accounting for government agencies. Perhaps he is best known in this regard for his years with the Tennessee Valley Authority (TVA) as its controller. He has also been credited with being in large measure responsible for the success of the Marshall Plan, the Economic Cooperation Administration.[1] In addition, he served on the staff of the Office of Emergency Management and War Production Board, was Executive Officer of the Petroleum Administration for War, Financial Advisor to the U. S. Secretary of Agriculture, Consultant to the U. S. General Accounting Office, member of the Excess Profits Tax Council of the U. S. Treasury and a member of the U. S. Chamber of Commerce Advisory Panel on Organization of Congress. His advice was also actively sought by the state of Illinois, where he worked closely with the State Auditor in preparing for reorganization of accounting practices in that state.

Among Kohler's major contributions in each of these capacities were his unflagging advocacy of an activity accounting system and his conviction that governmental accounting should differ in no material way from accounting in the private sector. This chapter contains an exploration of Kohler's contributions in the area of governmental accounting. It provides an examination of his activities at the Tennessee Valley Authority and particularly his installation of a system of activity accounting within that organization. The applicability of this responsibility accounting concept in other enterprises is then examined. In addition, Kohler's criticisms of Federal accounting and his specific suggestions for its improvement in the areas of budgeting, accountability, reporting, and the audit and control functions are detailed. Finally, the chapter addresses Kohler's position on the distinction between management and accounting and the role which accounting plays in enterprise management.

THE TENNESSEE VALLEY AUTHORITY

The Early Years

The Tennessee Valley Authority was established in 1933 to improve navigation, create flood controls, and provide hydroelectric power for the Tennessee River area. The TVA was given corporate powers and was operated under the jurisdiction of a board of three directors appointed by the President and approved by Congress. It was financed by Congressional appropriations, bonds, and revenue from the sale of power, fertilizer, and services.[2]

There had been numerous unsuccessful attempts to build a canal and install locks at Muscle Shoals, Alabama, and thereby to make the Tennessee River navigable. Under the TVA Act, a nine-foot channel was maintained between Knoxville and the Ohio River, making it possible for boats of some size to get as far as Knoxville, something they had previously been unable to do. Additionally, flood control was a major concern. Many people lived along the river's edge in substandard housing, and flooding each year washed away many of their possessions. A series of dams were used to keep the water at a nearly constant level. The provision of power was incidental to the flood-control question: the creation of a power facility meant that the impounded water could be put to good use.[3]

Highly qualified individuals were brought in to direct TVA activities. However, this diligence did not in general extend to the accounting staff.[4] Inadequate reporting led, by 1938, to Congressional concern about General Accounting Office (GAO) field audits which had resulted in reports containing thousands of exceptions to TVA practices.[5] However, many of these exceptions resulted from readily justifiable departures from prescribed procedure. For example, one complaint was of numerous instances where returnable monies received were not deposited in a special account. Jerry Stone, who was with the TVA during this period and later served on Kohler's staff as assistant controller, explained:

> The law referred to is a requirement that all returnable moneys received, such as bid bond deposits and other items of this nature, shall be identified and deposited in the U. S. Treasury, reimbursements to be made by Treasury check.
>
> The 'countless instances' were truly countless. They included nickel bottle deposits left by workmen at damsite commissaries. If a workman wanted to buy a bottled soft drink and take it off the premises, he would leave a nickel bottle deposit, which nickel was tossed into a cigar box, from which it was returned when the bottle came back.[6]

Kohler, too, was fascinated by the unimportant nature of the exceptions and characterized the conclusions drawn by the GAO staff as both fantastic and irresponsible.[7] He later recalled that the exceptions consisted of several volumes, collectively measuring nearly a foot high; and, although they had been regarded by the TVA board as ridiculous and therefore not worth its attention, they had been piling up over the years and by 1938 were becoming a matter of Congressional concern.[8]

Kohler as Comptroller

But the Authority's problems were larger than the GAO exceptions, and Eric Kohler was brought in, first as a consultant in 1937 and ultimately as comptroller in May of 1938. In addition to disposing of the GAO exceptions, reorganizing the accounting processes, and producing an intelligible set of financial statements, the new Comptroller's task included taking on the apparent multitude of TVA critics--including Congress, the Edison Electric Institute, the U. S. Chamber of Commerce, and the U. S. General Accounting Office--and allocating the Authority's massive joint and common costs.

Prior to his employment, Kohler had laid down certain conditions which would allow him to deal with these problems: he insisted that he be directly responsible to the TVA board of directors and that he be given a free hand in choosing personnel and in establishing accounting policy.[9] Within four months, aided by a group of fifty accountants from several public accounting firms, he reconstructed TVA transactions for a five-year period. Accounts were rewritten and financial statements, along with a lengthy narrative report, were prepared. Subsequently, he brought in a firm of independent public accountants who audited and gave an unqualified report on the Authority's first meaningful financial statements.[10]

Shortly after the new Comptroller's arrival at the TVA, a Joint Congressional Committee had been formed to investigate allegations against the Authority. In December, Kohler submitted the report to the Committee and provided a week-long testimony which quieted the Authority's critics, at least temporarily.[11] The testimony was not presented entirely without complications: on the day that the report of TVA's auditors, Lybrand, Ross Brothers and Montgomery, was submitted, the McKesson-Robbins scandal broke, and one senator threw his copy of the TVA report in the wastebasket saying "audits don't mean anything."[12] However, according to Kohler, the Committee came to understand the functions of accounting and auditing and accepted the report.[13]

Satisfying the Authority's critics was only a part of the task. Kohler was also charged with determining a method of allocating the Authority's joint and common costs among the three objectives: power, navigation, and flood control. These costs consisted of the dams, purchased land rights, the removal of trees and houses from prospective reservoirs, the construction of access roads to the lakes behind the dams, relocation of homes, and so forth.[14] Several methods of allocating these costs had been proposed by economists, engineers, and public-works consultants. Among them were: (1) vendibility theory, which was described as an allocation based on market prices less direct costs; (2) benefit theory, which involved allocation based on the worth or benefit deriving from services; (3) use-of-facilities theory, allocating common costs according to the use of water for each purpose; (4) equal-apportionment theory, allocating costs evenly among the three purposes; (5) direct-cost theory, which was based on direct costs of separable single-purpose items; (6) incremental-cost theory, which would result in minimum allocation to power since its production was, as specified by the TVA Act, decidedly secondary to navigation and flood control; (7) substitutive-power-cost theory, assigning expenses to power according to the alternative justifiable cost of a single-purpose power project reduced by the cost of direct power facilities; and (8) alternative-justifiable-cost theory, which involved computing the most economical alternative cost providing the same benefit in terms of each of the three purposes.[15] Several of these proposals involved measurement problems which prohibited their adoption. Proposals six and seven involved too small or too great a cost allocation to power. The alternative-justifiable-cost theory seemed to the TVA Financial Policy Committee to be the soundest of the proposals, and, although it was rejected, it was viewed as supporting the judgment basis which was ultimately adopted. The major criticism of the alternative-justifiable-cost theory was that it was based on the costs of three hypothetical systems, none of which actually existed.[16] Kohler viewed each of the proposals as having serious defects and ultimately pushed for the adoption of a judgment basis of allocation: 40 percent of the cost was allocated to power, 30 percent to navigation, and 30 percent to flood control.

Activity Accounting

As he approached the task of reorganizing the accounting system, Kohler found to his dismay that, although transactions had been painstakingly recorded, the records were in such a condition that they could not have been audited, and no financial statements had been produced.[17] Reports were not being used and, in fact, when they were suspended, only the file clerks noticed. Kohler set out to design a system characterized by simplicity, clearly defined lines of responsibility, and prompt, useful reporting. He did away with the allotment ledger, budgetary accounting, booking commitments and obligations. He abandoned the punched-card accounting system in favor of three National Bookkeeping machines. Decentralization and delegation of responsibility were essential, the goal being to see that the accounts would follow management, decentralizing where management was decentralized. Three primary offices were established: the main office in Knoxville, a power office in Chattanooga, and a fertilizer or chemical-engineering office at Muscle Shoals. In addition, an accounting office was set up at the location of each project. Finally, Kohler installed a series of activity accounts designed to foster management responsibility. He saw his job as defining each existing activity, delineating the authority given each activity head, and using budgeting, accounting, and reporting to help the activity head define and recognize his responsibility.[18] The goal again was simplicity and clearly defined responsibility. Prorations and allocations were to be avoided wherever possible. The organization's responsibilities were divided into projects and programs and were then further subdivided into the smallest possible units of cost and responsibility, the activities.

Basically, activity accounting is a responsibility accounting concept based on two fundamental ideas: (1) a person should not be held responsible for a cost over which he has no control, and (2) cost allocations and reallocations should be avoided wherever possible.[19] Kohler was, in fact, commissioned to write a monograph on responsibility accounting for Arthur Andersen & Co. Although the monograph never materialized activity accounting is well-documented. In presentations before various groups and in several articles as well as a lengthy discussion in A Dictionary for Accountants, Kohler explained the rationale behind and the basic tenets of activity accounting. For example, in an address to the Society for the Advancement of Management in 1943, he described the systems's components:

1. An AGENCY is any instrumentality of government which administers an appropriation or allotment. . . .

2. A DIVISION is any major assignment of control within an agency. . . .

3. A PROJECT is a major property-acquisition function of an agency, the costs of which are assets. . . .

4. A PROGRAM is a major operational function of an agency, often repetitive, the costs of which are expenses. . . .

5. SUBPROJECTS and SUBPROGRAMS are organizational, geographical, or other convenient breakdowns of projects and programs. . . .

6. An ORGANIZATIONAL UNIT, the smallest administrative subdivision of control, consists of one person, or one or more persons under a supervisor, engaged as a working group on one or more activities.

7. An ACTIVITY represents the lowest practicable coincident level of function, management, budgeting and accounting. . . .

8. An organizational unit may be charged with a number of activities but an activity may not extend beyond a single organizational unit. . . .

9. One or more accounts should be maintained for each activity. . . . No one account is permitted to go beyond an organizational unit as herein defined. . . .

10. One combination of activity accounts will yield financial statements of projects or programs; another, overall statements of organizational costs.

11. One breakdown of an activity account will yield expenditures by objects; another, unit costs.

12. A budget is the sum total of activity costs, with subtotals by projects and programs, or subtotals by major organizations. . . .[20]

TVA's several thousand activities, as defined above, were described in the Authority's accounting manual. Each was provided a quarter-page or half-page description which included expenditure limitations and activity identification. Accounts relating to each activity were maintained. A record of each month's transactions was submitted to each activity supervisor by the fifth of the following month. The supervisor reviewed the report and passed it on to a supervisory authority who likewise reviewed and shared responsibility for the operation of the unit. Thus costs were summarized at each successively higher supervisory level rather than allocated to the individual activities. The budget, likewise, was based upon the activity accounts and linked to management responsibility for the accounts. Any idea that budgets could be handed down from above was abandoned. Kohler was convinced that the focus on the smallest unit of function, budgeting, and accounting--the activity, accompanied by commensurate delegations of authority and responsibility--resulted in the greatest degree of control over expenditures and operations.[21]

Kohler and the TVA's Critics

Kohler's tenure with the TVA began amid criticism of the Authority by Congress and the GAO, and his testimony before the Joint Congressional Committee marked only a temporary truce and not the end of his confrontations with TVA critics. For example, in 1940 the Chicago Tribune carried editorials calling for an audit of the Authority by independent accountants and questioning the TVA's allocations.[22] The Tribune concluded that the largest share of TVA's common costs should be allocated to power and that a "thoroly [sic] skeptical audit" would be an important first step in making the TVA more responsive to the public. Kohler defended the Authority's allocation practices and reminded the paper's readers that independent audits of the TVA had been made in each of the preceding two years by Lybrand, Ross Brothers and Montgomery, whom Kohler termed "thoroughgoing skeptics."[23]

Even after he left the TVA, Kohler continued to be its defender. He entered into an exchange of letters between E. Arnold Sunstrom, who had followed Kohler as TVA Comptroller, and Leonard Spacek of Arthur Andersen & Co. Spacek had criticized the Authority for not providing a charge against income for the payment of interest on the part of its power investment financed from Congressional appropriations. Kohler's reply (to Sunstrom) was that, since interest was not incurred by the TVA, its recognition as a construction cost or as an operating expense would be artificial and arbitrary and not consistent with good commercial accounting practices. Since the TVA was financed by Congressional appropriations, the Federal government was in effect providing equity capital, and an interest charge on noninterest-bearing equity funds would be inappropriate. Spacek's argument was that, since the United States government was paying interest on obligations which it had incurred at least in part to finance TVA operations, that interest charge should be passed on to the TVA.[24] This same question had been raised in 1945 in a

GAO report, and Kohler had at that time composed a lengthy reply to T. Coleman Andrews, Director of the GAO Corporation Audits Division, pointing out that, since no interest expense had been incurred, none should be charged against operations.[25]

He also defended the TVA against a 1950 attack made by Representative Norris Poulson in a speech before the American Institute of Accountants.[26] The interest question was again included in the charges, along with attacks on TVA classification, allocation, and accounting methods. Again Kohler's reply was that no interest expense had been incurred. He also pointed out that TVA account classification closely followed Federal Power Commission (FPC) standards, that allocation procedures had been carefully studied and had been approved by the FPC, and that TVA accounting conformed to accounting standards of private businesses.

In general, he called charges such as those by Spacek, Poulson, and the GAO improperly researched and ill-founded, and he readily seized the opportunity to defend the accounting procedures which he had established at the TVA.

GOVERNMENTAL ACCOUNTING

Public vs. Private Sector Accounting

Kohler was dismayed at the state of governmental accounting and expressed the conviction that an appropriate solution to the deficiencies was for government agencies to adopt accounting practices similar to those followed in the commercial sector. He argued that "costs are the same everywhere, and government stands to gain if the well-developed notions of cost accountants can be adopted to the Federal picture."[27] He enumerated the structural parallels in a report for the Illinois State Auditor. He compared the general public to corporate stockholders who determine the functions of the government or business and who supply tax monies or capital. He equated legislators to boards of directors: both devise policies for the agencies; and he compared the President or governor to the corporate chief executive officer. He viewed reporting and accounting for performance as needs which were the same for both public and private entities.[28] He described himself as one of those accountants who believed that the differences were not significant and as one who hoped that governmental officials would learn the language of businessmen.[29] Not content to make sweepingly general criticisms, Kohler specifically listed what he believed were some major difficulties: (1) the booking of budgets and encumbrances; (2) poorly devised classifications of accounts, particularly a noticeable failure to distinguish between capital and revenue expenditures; (3) failure to understand and fix the account unit; and (4) the absence of reports which provide an analysis of costs of services and a measure of service accomplishments. Among the solutions which he recommended were the establishment of an extensive audit function, the installation of a system of responsibility accounting, and the appointment of a controller for each spending agency.[30] The following sections contain a discussion of each of these areas of concern.

The Budget

One of the major problems in governmental accounting, Kohler believed, was the booking of budgets and encumbrances. The practice, which had evolved from a desire to ensure that legislative limitations on expenditures would not be exceeded, had become cumbersome. Kohler proposed instead the use of a memorandum budget ledger so that encumbrances were noted but did not actually enter the accounts. Under his scheme, encumbered amounts would be noted on small cards. The information would be readily available so that periodic reports could be set up in three columns: one for expenditures, one for encumbrances, and one for budgetary limits. The accounts thereby retain a singleness of purpose, uncomplicated by committed but unexpended amounts, and the budgeting and expenditure processes are simplified.[31]

The responsibility for seeing that budgetary limitations are not exceeded belongs to management. The budget is not an accounting device at all but is an instrument of managerial control. As such, it has no place in the accounts.[32] Kohler did not question the need for budgetary controls. What he questioned was their incorporation in the accounting system:

> Budgetary control begins with the persons charged with a spending program, not with the accounting records. . . . Where careless administrative methods are in effect, the most elaborate bookkeeping records will not prevent commitments beyond permissive amounts.[33]

The budget can contribute to careful administration. It is a means of forcing activity heads to come before the agency manager and justify their programs and of giving the manager a basis for allocating resources among activities. The administrator must periodically reappraise the activities under his control and, after budget approval, is provided a means of controlling and reviewing the extent to which policies have been carried out.[34]

Classification of Accounts

An important problem is account classification which fails to distinguish between capital and revenue expenditures. Accounts should follow private sector practices so that financial statements will be more useful and will reveal the costs of the assets which the federal government possesses.[35]

Accountability

A responsibility accounting system is essential. Delegation of authority, responsibility, and accountability must be fortified by accounts which provide cost information by organizational unit. Groupings of accounts by funds, allocations relating to the performance of a service by one organization for another, and distribution of overhead contribute only to confusion.[36]

Kohler's suggestion was the installation of an activity accounting system. Programs are divided into subprograms and are further subdivided by activities. Accounts are organized by activity; responsibility for each activity is firmly delegated and rests with the activity head; and costs are summarized upward rather than allocated and prorated downward. The budget is initiated at the activity level; it is not handed down from above. Kohler's argument was that the activity head is the authority on costs relating to his activity. Budget figures are working controls related to the organizational unit.[37] Therefore, the activity head must play a primary role in the planning and budgeting process. The budget contains "activity proposals for the coming year and a plan for putting them into effect."[38] Once approved, the budget must be broken down by organizational unit and further broken down by object of expenditure. The job of administering the budget then rests with the head of the organizational unit. Periodic reports to activity heads provide the means of measuring the success with which the designated responsibility has been met. Expense accounting is centered on each activity or area of responsibility, and the various layers of operation and supervision are supplied with whatever details of performance are desired.[39]

The activity becomes the smallest subdivision of function, budgeting, and accounting. In the expenditure accounts for each activity appear direct, variable costs over which the activity head has control. The agency head must then place in the hands of each activity head the authority and the responsibility associated with his subdivision of operations. [40]

Reporting

An important part of an activity accounting system is prompt, periodic reporting which enables each manager to review the costs for which he is responsible and to appraise his unit's performance. [41]

At the Tennessee Valley Authority, Kohler had replaced the existing reporting system with one designed to provide no more in the way of reports than would actually be used. This approach involved extensive study aimed at discovering what information should be included. The report, he claimed, had to be geared to the individual. "When you get out reports," he told a group of government accountants and internal auditors, "remember that they are not the type of thing that anybody can produce."

> They have to be designed with the thought in mind
> that you are giving them to an individual or group
> for review, for understanding, for action; and
> that, as individuals or groups change, your report
> may have to take on a different form and content.
> In other words, what you are preparing is something
> personal, something the individual can digest,
> something he can understand; and proof of this is
> to talk to him about it. Find out what he gets out
> of the report; what he seems to be most concerned
> about. It may be that you have left something out
> of that report that is important to him.[42]

Of course, there may be information that the individual needs

but does not request, information that he does not yet

understand how to use. In that case, the accountant may have

to do a selling and teaching job so that the activity head

can effectively carry out his responsibilities. The goal is

a simple, as well as an individualized, approach. Under the

TVA activity accounting system, reported transactions during

the month and a cumulative total of those transactions were

printed on plain, untitled paper. A record of the month's

transactions was submitted to each activity supervisor by the

fifth of the following month. The report was to be signed

and a copy returned by the tenth. Failure to return or

correct the report indicated acceptance of the charges as

presented. These reports were essential elements of the

responsibility accounting concept. Kohler saw no reason why

such reporting could not be adopted by other governmental

entities.[43]

Control

Kohler advocated the installation of an extensive internal audit function headed by a controller and fortified by a vigilant internal auditor. Each organizational unit is responsible for a preaudit, or voucher audit, which involves an examination of creditor's invoices, payrolls, and other claims before payment. Preaudit assures that expenditures have been properly authorized; that goods received were ordered by a properly authorized individual and that they agree in quantity, quality, and price with purchase order specifications; and that the billed amount has been charged to the appropriate account. The preaudit is an essential part of expenditure control. It is to be accompanied by a procedural audit, which is an examination of internal controls and other procedures by an external auditor. The procedural audit includes the examination of operating procedures and compares performance with prescribed standards.[44] A third audit function, the postaudit, includes the traditional audit function performed by an external auditor, but the term may also be used to refer to an examination by an internal auditor. The latter function is, however, more appropriately called an internal audit. [45]

Kohler believed that the function of the internal auditor was a vitally important one, and he urged the person in this capacity to work for organizational and operational improvement and to act as the conscience and moral leader of the agency he served.[46] The internal auditor is responsible for reviewing policies, procedures, and transactions; for testing the accuracy of records; and for seeing that operations are efficient and economical. [47]

The effectiveness of the internal auditor depends on a sound organizational structure which includes a responsibility accounting system and a management which recognizes the interdependence of authority, responsibility, and accountability. These elements are the framework of the organizational structure. The internal auditor then continually tests that structure to see that it is operating properly and that management policies are being implemented. It is his job to review expenditure controls at the point at which the expenditure decision is made; to review increases in expenditures; to test purchasing activities, questioning prices and quantities; and to provide reports which are written in a clear, nontechnical manner. [48]

The internal auditor should never be more than one step removed from the organizational or agency head. Ideally, he should report to the contoller who, in turn, reports directly to the administrative head of the agency.

The controller is a vital part of each governmental unit. According to Kohler, "Except for the smallest agencies, a professionally qualified controller [should] be employed."[49] He should be instructed in the law and regulations which affect his agency's disbursing and other accounting procedures. He is responsible for accounting policy, methods, and procedure; for reviewing and refining internal reports to insure that they meet user needs; and for aiding the budgeting and administrative auditing process.[50]

The controller, as Kohler described him, "sits on top of the financial picture."[51] He should assist in forming and enforcing financial policies, should establish internal accounting policies, and should be familiar with organizational problems and management devices. He should have both the authority and the willingness to take immediate action where it is needed.[52] Kohler viewed the controller's function as a broadly defined and demanding one, and he suggested that the American Institute should maintain a list of qualified individuals from which the governmental agencies could draw.

ACCOUNTING AND MANAGEMENT

Accounting provides the means to make management control possible, but the ultimate responsibility rests with qualified individuals. To assume that one can create a well-run organization simply by legislatively requiring certain bookkeeping devices is, at best, naive. Expenditure controls rest with individuals vested with the authority and responsibility for planning and incurring the expenditures. Accounting techniques make possible these necessary delegations of authority.[53] Thus accounting is necessary to, but not a substitute for, sound management practices.

Because management does much of its thinking and communicating in terms of accounting, the accountant provides an important service to management in its planning and decision-making processes. The accountant, for example, provides cost information, but management must decide how to allocate those costs to the production process. Expenditure controls, too, are a management responsibility. Booking budgets and encumbrances assigns a management-related function to accounting and goes beyond the appropriate interrelationship of the two functions. Accounting provides the information which enables management to gauge the extent to which its budget objectives are being met, but it is not designed to serve as a substitute for management.[54]

SUMMARY

In governmental agencies, as well as in the private sector, it is essential that the requisite degrees of authority, responsibility, and accountability be incorporated into a system of responsibility accounting. Such a system includes a well-devised classification of accounts; a clear designation of the account unit; prompt, periodic reports which provide cost-of-services information; an extensive audit function; and the installation of a controller for each agency. These practices were a part of the activity accounting system which Kohler established at the Tennessee

Valley Authority, and they are practices which he continued to emphasize in later writing, speaking, and consulting engagements.

He believed that governmental accounting should differ in no material way from accounting in the private sector, and, in the installation of an activity accounting system at the Tennessee Valley Authority, he worked to incorporate what he saw as the best in commercial accounting practice. He subdivided programs and projects into their smallest subunits, which he deemed activities. A designated individual was then made responsible for each activity. Accounts and reports were activity oriented, and the budgeting process began at the activity level. Kohler then brought in independent certified public accountants to review the financial statements of the organization, again following the practices of the commercial sector.

He encouraged all governmental agencies to adopt similar practices. He urged the abandonment of the practice of booking budgets and encumbrances. He argued for the adoption of responsibility accounting and against allocations and prorations wherever they could be avoided. The direct costs of each activity should be assembled in periodic reports specifically designed for the activity head. Finally, he emphasized the installation of appropriate controls to insure that the organizational structure worked in the way in which it was intended to work.

NOTES

[1]Samuel Nakasian, "Eric Kohler in the Marshall Plan," in Eric Louis Kohler: Accounting's Man of Principles, W. W. Cooper and Yuji Ijiri, editors (Reston, Virginia: Reston Publishing Company, 1979), pp. 98-113.

[2]Eric L. Kohler, "The TVA and its Power Accounting Problems," Accounting Review (January, 1948), p. 45.

[3]Eric L. Kohler, Tennessee Valley Authority Oral History (Memphis, Tennessee: Memphis State University Oral History Research Office, February, 1971), Interview #2, pp. 1-16.

[4]Jerry F. Stone, "Eric L. Kohler, Comptroller of the Tennessee Valley Authority," in Eric Louis Kohler: Accounting's Man of Principles, Cooper and Ijiri, editors, p. 84.

[5]According to W. O. Heffernan, who summarized GAO audit findings for the Joint Congressional Committee investigating the Tennessee Valley Authority, "exceptions do not mean that there has been any shortage or fraud; nor do they mean even that there have been expenditures which the General Accounting Office believes not justified by applicable statutes. They mean only that the General Accounting Office questions certain disbursements and desires further information concerning them. It should be noted that the taking of exceptions precedes any determination that disbursements are or are not justified. When further information is received, the exceptions may be and usually are removed." Furthermore, when an exception is taken, it is taken in the total amount of the voucher and not simply in that part of the voucher which relates specifically to the item in question. The result, as noted by the Committee in its conclusions, is "to give the impression that vast sums of the Authority's money have been misapplied" when in fact the actual errors are much smaller than published GAO findings would indicate. Thus, to one unfamiliar with GAO methods, it appears that TVA personnel are guilty of massive shortages or fraudulent dealings. From: U. S., Congress, Senate, Report of the Joint Committee on the Investigation of the Tennessee Valley Authority, S. Doc. 56, 76th Cong., 1st sess., 1939, pt. 2, pp. 24-25 and 131.

[6]Stone, p. 85.

[7]Kohler, TVA Oral History, pp. 8-10.

[8]Ibid.

[9]Ibid., p. 3.

[10]Stone, p. 88. The report did contain an exception regarding allocations related to the interpretation of the Tennessee Valley Authority Act.

[11]The Joint Committee's final report indicates that they were satisfied with Kohler's reorganization and reporting efforts. The report of the Committee's auditor testifies to this fact and confirms the extent of the contribution which Kohler made at the TVA. He reported that TVA accounting had been unsatisfactory up until the time that Kohler was employed. Subsequent to his engagement as comptroller, however, conditions improved: "The financial statements issued as volume II of Tennessee Valley Authority's Annual Report for the fiscal year ending June 30, 1938, indicate a sharp departure from prior Tennessee Valley Authority financial reporting. Commercial reporting methods have been followed, the allocation of costs between multiple purposes has been fully reflected, and full straight-line depreciation has been taken on all limited life assets. The fact that the accuracy of the statements has been certified to by an independent accounting firm of unquestioned competency rendered unnecessary any other auditing confirmation." From: Report of the Joint Committee, p. 26.

[12]Kohler, TVA Oral History, Interview #1, p. 32.

[13]Ibid. Kohler says that Francis Biddle, attorney for the Committee, "did a masterful job of describing the function of auditing and the worth of audit reports."

[14]Ibid., p. 13.

[15]Testimony prepared by Eric L. Kohler in the Spring of 1947 for presentation to the Senate Public Works Committee in connection with S. 1277. Typewritten.

[16]Ibid., pp. 23-24.

[17]Eric L. Kohler, "Accounting for the T.V.A." Accounting Forum (June, 1941), p. 49.

[18]Kohler, TVA Oral History, Interview #1, pp. 35-36.

[19]Stone, p. 91.

[20]Eric L. Kohler, "The Activity as a Basis for Fiscal Control in the TVA," Typewritten address, 17 November 1943.

[21]Ibid.

[22]Chicago Tribune, 3 January 1940, and 18 February 1940.

[23]Eric L. Kohler, Letter to the editor of the Chicago Tribune, 26 February 1940.

[24]Letter from Leonard Spacek to E. Arnold Sunstrom, 28 December 1949; Letter from Eric Kohler to E. Arnold Sunstrom, 6 January 1950.

[25]Letter from Eric Kohler to T. Coleman Andrews, 11 September 1946.

[26]Letter from Eric Kohler to Representative Norris Poulson, 22 February 1950.

[27]Eric L. Kohler, "Deficiencies in Federal Accounting," Accounting Review (September, 1940), p. 443.

[28]Eric L. Kohler, "Notes on Fiscal Reorganization in the State of Illinois." Typewritten notes prepared at the request of Lloyd Morey, State Auditor, August, 1956.

[29]Eric L. Kohler, "Accounting for Municipally Owned Assets." Typewritten address presented before the Municipal Finance Officers Association, undated.

[30]Eric L. Kohler, "Accounting Progress in the Federal Government," Illinois Society of CPAs Bulletin (September, 1945), p. 11.

[31]Kohler, "Deficiencies in Federal Accounting," p. 444.

[32]Ibid.

[33]Eric L. Kohler, "Need for Budgetary Accounts," Accounting Review (December, 1940), p. 530.

[34]Eric L. Kohler, "The Role of Accounting in the Development of Administrative Techniques." Typewritten, undated, p. 5.

[35]Kohler, "Deficiencies in Federal Accounting," p. 444.

[36]Ibid., p. 445.

[37]Eric L. Kohler, "The Activity: Nerve Center of Management and Accounting," N.A.C.A. Bulletin (August, 1955), p. 1628.

[38]Kohler, "The Role of Accounting in the Development of Administrative Techniques," p. 2.

[39]Eric L. Kohler, "Notes on Activity Accounting," International Journal of Accounting, Education and Research (Spring, 1967), p. 60.

[40]Ibid.

[41]Eric L. Kohler, "Basic Concepts in the Reorganization of State Accounting and Auditing Practices," The Illinois Certified Public Accountant (Winter, 1956-57), p. 8.

[42]Eric L. Kohler, "An Outsider Looks at the GAO Manual." Typewritten address before a joint meeting of the Dayton chapters of the Federal Government Accountants Association and the Institute of Internal Auditors, 26 February 1959.

[43]Eric L. Kohler, "Accounting for the T.V.A." Accounting Forum (June, 1941), pp. 49-50.

[44]Kohler, "Basic Concepts in the Reorganization of State Accounting and Auditing Practices," p. 9.

[45]Ibid.

[46]Eric L. Kohler, "Essential Elements in a Program of Internal Audit," The Federal Accountant (January, 1952), p. 15.

[47]Kohler, "Basic Concepts in the Reorganization of State Accounting and Auditing Practices," p. 9.

[48]Kohler, "Essential Elements in a Program of Internal Audit," pp. 12-13.

[49]Eric L. Kohler, "Accounting Practices in State Agencies," Journal of Accountancy (August, 1959), p. 58.

[50]Ibid., pp. 58-59.

[51]Letter from Eric Kohler to Mr. Corson, 30 January 1945.

[52]Ibid.

[53]Eric L. Kohler, "Accounting Practices in State Agencies," p. 60; and "Background for Management Accounting Techniques," N.A.A. Bulletin (October, 1961), p. 9.

[54]Kohler, "Deficiencies in Federal Accounting," p. 444.

VII
THE PROFESSION

Eric Kohler has been referred to as the conscience of the accounting profession,[1] and those who knew him can understand how he earned such a title. He was a man dedicated to a highly principled approach to professional standards and one who was impatient with compromise. He was, in fact, outspoken and unyielding on matters of principle. He was convinced that the profession must be guided by standards which promote full disclosure and minimize the possibility of manipulation in the presentation of financial information. He insisted on clear, direct communication and was intolerant of vague, meaningless terms which allow compromise positions or which obscure meaning. These characteristics--his impatience with compromise, his highly principled approach, and his insistence on full, informative disclosure and straightforward communication--would seem to make him well-fitted for a role as the profession's conscience.

And it is a role he seems to have accepted readily. From his position as editor of the Accounting Review, he surveyed professional activities and quickly pointed out what he saw as weaknesses in publications or in positions taken. In fact, he believed that it was the editor's job to review and comment on such developments and to expose accountants to new ideas.[2] Other articles and correspondence also provide evidence of his vigilance in monitoring professional developments.

These writings indicate his insistence on high principles and his impatience with what he saw as professional complacency. Accountants, he believed, should continually strive to improve practice through adopting theoretically sound positions and avoiding compromise. They should refuse to be satisfied with the state of the art at any point in time. They should recognize their obligations to third persons and acknowledge and work to solve the problems facing them. Primary among those problems were:

1. The failure of the profession to accept its responsibility to society at large and to third party financial statement users in particular. The certified public accountant, as indicated by his very title, has profound obligations to third persons and should not attempt to limit his responsibility or liability where they are concerned.

2. The promulgation of professional standards which evidenced insufficient research and sacrificed good

theory for the sake of expediency. Kohler's criticism in this area was directed toward the American Institute of Accountants and its standard-setting bodies, the Committee on Accounting Procedure and the Accounting Principles Board.

3. The failure to prepare accountants to accept their professional role. Kohler believed that accountants could not be adequately prepared by Schools of Business. Instead a separate professional school of accountancy is necessary. In addition, professional examinations need to be more carefully screened.

This chapter contains an examination of Kohler's positions in each of these problem areas. Those positions have been extracted from the editorial pages of the Accounting Review and from other Kohler articles and correspondence.

AUDITOR'S RESPONSIBILITY

In a March, 1931, Accounting Review editorial, Kohler classified accountants' problems as social and internal. The social problems relate to the accountant's duty and responsibility to the public. The internal problems relate to ethics, education, and a body of theory which remains a few steps ahead of society's demands. He condemned the efforts of accounting professionals to cloak their reports in language designed more to protect themselves than to inform the reader. He believed they should accept unlimited liability for their judgments and should not rely on attorneys to tell them how far their responsibility extended.[3] He believed the accountant had profound obligations to the public and that it was in the recognition of these obligations that he earned the title "certified public accountant." He expected the profession ultimately to raise the level of honesty and fair practice in business.[4] Sound practice based on these considerations then could become the basis for accounting education; and accounting educators, by concentrating on the larger picture, could contribute significantly to accounting practice.

Liability to Third Parties

Kohler contended that the term public accountant denoted responsibilities to third persons, the recognition of which was the auditor's best protection against personal liability for negligence. The accountant, although employed by management, is responsible to the world. Kohler's 1934 editorial entitled "A Nervous Profession" was his strongest statement of impatience with the profession's self-satisfied approach. In that writing he attacked accountants for failing to recognize their obligations to third persons. He had earlier cited this failure as a major difficulty: in 1931 he had described both accounting theory and practice as drifting hopelessly as the profession ignored the social implications of its professional endeavors. At that time he suggested that a fruitful research topic might well be the orientation of accountancy as a social science.

He was appalled at the idea that accountants would carry insurance or incorporate to limit their liability: "No worse contravention," he said, "of their duties to third persons could be conceived."[5] Liability, he believed, should not be limited. Responsibility must be recognized.

The accountant can best recognize his obligations and protect himself by seeking to inform and safeguard the investor.[6] If a business offers its securities to the public, it is obligated to provide complete information to potential investors. The fear of helping competitors is not sufficient justification for concealing facts.[7] The auditor stands in an ideal position to protect the public from unscrupulous practices on the part of those issuing financial statements, either in an initial offering of securities or at regular intervals during the life of the business entity.

Kohler was shocked by the Ultramares case,[8] contending that a review of the facts led one to the conclusion that either there was collusion between the accountants and management or that the accountants' work was not adequately supervised or reviewed. In either case, he believed the conclusion drawn by the court might well have been fraud.[9] He said, however, that the results of the case should ultimately be salutary to the profession by making accountants more keenly aware of their responsibilities to third persons.

The Audit Report

One way in which Kohler believed accountants had tried to limit their liability was by careful wording of the audit report. He complained that audit reports were frequently not understood by their readers. As a result, sound investment and credit decisions were jeopardized. He responded to the suggestion that the certificate read "We hereby certify to you" by saying that, if the accountant wished thus to limit his obligation to third persons, he should label himself a private rather than a public accountant and should issue no certificate at all.

His conclusion in the Ultramares case was that much of the problem lay in the meaningless verbiage of the audit certificate. He criticized "We hereby certify that, in our opinion" not only as representing too many words but also as leaving the exact meaning of the certification open to speculation. Why not, he asked, simply say "We believe"? The understanding of the layman would thereby be enhanced, and the interests of simplicity and clarity would be served.[10] Better yet, he contended, would be to say only "Approved" or "Approved, with the following qualifications" followed by the firm's name and the designation "Certified

Public Accountants."

An Expanded Role

Kohler firmly believed that the accountant should have as his objective the good of society. Accounting information lends itself to use for social purposes. By measuring costs and providing reports which can be related to wages, prices, and budgeting, the accountant can contribute to intelligent competition and general social welfare.

As the accountant embraces his broader social responsibilities, his role will increase. Kohler envisioned him as a business advisor in the formation, combination, and dissolution of corporations; as one who promotes good financial practice urging full disclosure; as an agent of the stockholders; as mediator between capital and labor; and as arbitrator between debtor and creditor.[11] By accepting these obligations, the accountant acknowledges his primary obligation to the public.

DEVELOPMENT OF STANDARDS

The American Institute of Accountants

A Gentlemen's Club

Kohler blasted the accounting profession for its organizational and standard-setting shortfalls. He was especially critical of professionals for failing to organize effectively to solve the problems which confronted them. The pages of the Accounting Review indicate his frustration with the American Institute of Accountants (AIA), an organization which he was convinced had an inflated opinion of its own importance. He encouraged accountants to question themselves and their motives, and he was impatient with anything he saw as self-laudatory. For example, when the AIA published Facts and Purposes, he described the Institute as possessing "a snobbishness and lack of good taste that have their origin in a real ignorance of the things at stake in the accounting profession."[12] An individual influenced by Durand W. Springer, leader of the rival American Society of Certified Public Accountants (ASCPA), and not kindly inclined to the AIA, Kohler called that group a "static, supremely self-satisfied organization, unashamed to tell the world how good it is, and not afraid to stretch and overstress facts in order to prove a point."[13]

Years later he recalled the AIA as determined to "maintain the even tenor of its function as a gentlemen's club," a determination which he was convinced was not conducive to the Institute's contributing significantly to the development of accounting principles.[14] At another time Kohler presented an individual who must surely have been an AIA member: Mr. MacMurdie, a fictional character who appears in a 1935 dialogue, is convinced that the primary function of a national organization of accountants is to provide the opportunity for professionals to get together to behave as gentlemen toward one another[15]; regulation is better left to others (specifically the Securities and Exchange Commission). Mr. Bardley, the character who seems to represent the author's viewpoint, disagrees. He believes that the profession has a responsibility to govern itself and that accountants should not be content to let those outside the profession do their thinking for them. If the profession is responsive to its social obligations, it will have little need for outside regulation.

Professional Pronouncements

Kohler was unhappy with the standard-setting efforts of the AIA. He viewed the development of a better-defined body of standards as a necessary step in the growth of the profession. As a member of the American Society of Certified Public Accountants, he had urged accountants to undertake "a scientific reconstruction of . . . theory and practice."[16] He recommended the establishment of a committee supported by the two national organizations, the ASCPA and the AIA. This committee would be charged with the responsibility for creating definitions and setting standards, for constructing uniform procedures and laws, for working to improve accounting education, and for developing a code of ethics based on the fundamental ideas of honor and fair play.[17] The report which contained this recommendation represents one of his earlier attempts to encourage professionals to make an organized effort to engage in meaningful research aimed at the development of improved standards and procedures.

Over the years he continued to stress the importance of organized research efforts.[18] As discussed in chapter four, Kohler found the American Institute of Accountants' (subsequently the American Institute of Certified Public Accountants) attempts at standard setting inadequate. In that chapter reference was made to some of his published comments on AIA publications. For example, he reviewed Audits of Corporate Accounts and concluded that, although it had revealed certain weaknesses in the profession, it had not provided the kind of standardization that he believed was necessary.[19] He also criticized the effects on income measurement of certain procedures advocated or permitted by the Committee on Accounting Procedure (CAP): charges to surplus, last-in-first-out inventory measurement, and accelerated depreciation methods. Kohler's letters reveal further criticism of professional pronouncements. At one point he noted that "the APB continues to grind out agonized copy on 'principles': compromised stuff emerging from widely differing opinions of Board and staff members."[20] Kohler's criticism was primarily that the public was being forgotten in this agonized effort. For example, in relation to Opinion No. 29, he complained:

> By the time its tortured language reaches the public the Board will have succeeded only in confusing the profession, to say nothing of the public. The latter audience is being given no more than a token consideration. The expectation seems to be that the public, to comprehend the meaning of 'asset,' will have to review (and understand) befuddled APB pronouncements, or to take the accountant's 'certified values' as gospel. In neither case can this possibly happen--as I am sure certain APB members are aware.[21]

In another letter (this time regarding APB Opinion No. 2) he had admitted: "Part of my bias in this matter arises from my conviction that today information to investors has ceased to be the foremost purpose of published financial statements and of annual reports. . . ."[22] In these areas, as in others, Kohler was concerned that financial information be presented in a manner that would be useful to third persons. When he perceived a failure on the part of standard setters to be responsive to user needs, he did not hesitate to remark bitingly on the pronouncements' deficiencies.

A further example of this criticism is provided by his comment on deferred taxes. In a 1967 letter he referred to the Accounting Principles Board (APB) release on accounting for income taxes as "nothing short of a major calamity in the orderly development of accounting and financial practices."[23] Of course, Kohler's opinion of the depth of clear thinking which had gone into the making of a pronouncement was certainly influenced by whether he agreed with the conclusion. In this case, his own opinion was that "the whole idea of tax deferral should be abolished" since it considers a "purely hypothetical contingent future expense" as a current expense and liability.[24]

He also wrote to a member of the APB regarding what he considered "the outlandish interpretation of the 'investment credit.'"[25] He regarded the cost reduction treatment of the credit as "a revival of the old manipulative processes (charges to surplus and surplus reserves, the creation of 'secret' reserves, and later such devices as deferred taxes)."[26]

Another attack was directed toward the earnings per share treatment outlined by the APB. Kohler called the means of averaging outstanding shares additional evidence of "tortured accounting," which is "accounting concocted by trucklers to intriguing arithmetic formulas containing unexplored, uncritically accepted hypotheses (a classic example: APBO 8)."[27] Earnings per share, Kohler contended, is a function of a moment in time, and the only significant number of shares is the number outstanding at the end of the period. The opinion, he concluded, was too much concerned with computations and not enough with practical meaning and application.[28]

It is clear that the APB frequently fell short of the goal which Kohler believed it should pursue--that is, to work toward a unified body of standards which would provide guidance for accountants and facilitate communication with those outside the profession. He also reviewed other AIA publications and pointed out what he saw as their shortcomings. Some of his comments on publications of the Committee on Accounting Procedure have been mentioned. A further example is provided by an editorial dealing with the CAP's Accounting Research Bulletins 1, 2, and 3 and the Institute's "Extensions of Auditing Procedure." Kohler reviewed these publications and concluded that they "gave no evidence of extensive research nor of well-reasoned conclusions":

> They reflect, on the other hand, a hasty marshalling of facts and opinions, and the derivation of temporizing rules to which it is doubtless hoped that a professional majority will subscribe. As models of approach in a field already heavily burdened with expedients and dogmatism, they leave much to be desired.[29]

Kohler distrusted the Committee on Accounting Procedure because he was convinced that it was geared to the support of the acts of practitioners to such an extent that it could ultimately be rallied to any of their current causes, even if the cause, such as value-related adjustments to accounting records, lacked theoretical support.[30] Of course, he never really forgave the Committee for its stand in favor of the current operating performance income statement. He considered such conclusions an indication of insufficient research. He suggested that future pronouncements be preceded by a complete consideration of the arguments pro and con, that related literature be acknowledged and discussed, and that opposing ideas be more thoroughly considered.[31]

He subsequently saw some progress being made. In a later article, he reviewed seven bulletins of the Committee on Auditing Procedure and found they had made a good start and indicated increased attention to fundamental objectives.[32]

Kohler believed that the AIA, at any rate, was not the appropriate body to lead the way in formulating accounting principles. The Institute, he perceived, frequently fell short in developing accounting theory because of the expedients which practitioners were often prevailed upon to adopt and because practitioners frequently failed to recognize the broader social implications of accounting.[33] Such shortsightedness was then reflected in publications which showed evidence of insufficient research. He criticized some of the publications for sacrificing good theory for the sake of expediency. For example, amortizing bond discount over the life of an old (now refunded) bond issue was chosen over the theoretically preferable immediate charge-off because the latter approach could significantly decrease reported net income in the year of refunding.

However, some of his strongest criticism of AIA publications was directed at proposals which were significantly different from current practice. Those proposals were the ones contained in Accounting Research Study (ARS) No. 1, "The Basic Postulates of Accounting," and ARS No. 3, "A Tentative Set of Broad Accounting Principles for Business Enterprises." Kohler attacked the proposals of these studies, stating that they gave no indication of research but were designed only to justify unjustifiable current value adjustments. His criticism was strong:

> "Research studies" 1 and 3 (in which no research was evident) had as their obvious purpose the justification of fixed-asset revaluations; and the absurd olio of "postulates" and "principles"--supported only by references to the scribblings of a small academic clique whose preconceived ideas on this subject were well-known--was a sad performance, indeed. That certain officers of the Institute, whose slants in the direction of a higher depreciation base for tax purposes were of long standing, had "planted" this clique to serve their purposes as an Institute mouthpiece is a still sadder commentary on the present competence of the Institute to provide an environment for research, let alone for formulating principles.[34]

In submitting his remarks on these studies to the Journal of Accountancy for publication, Kohler noted that "Mason, Moonitz, and Sprouse are fine chaps but their pseudo-research effluvia (here I would include Bulletin 3, also) have set the Institute back a couple of decades."[35] He suggested that future research efforts should incorporate present standards and the reasons supporting them, should develop a historical background, and should present and discuss opposing points of view. Finally, such conclusions as would then be reached should be labeled <u>proposals</u> and not <u>principles</u>.[36] Interestingly enough, Kohler's proposals for improving research efforts at this too-theoretical end of the spectrum parallel those he made for studies at the too-expedient end: all sides of the argument are to be discussed; related literature is to be acknowledged; and opposing ideas are to be considered.

Research efforts, in brief, should then be carefully and painstakingly pursued, and all sides of the issue must be thoroughly considered. Only then can a research program be expected to make a real contribution to professional growth.

The American Accounting Association

Kohler measured the AIA's attempts to accept its responsibility as a national organization and as a leader in the development of standards and found them lacking. The American Accounting Association (AAA), on the other hand, he viewed as having cultivated a greater awareness of the things at stake in the profession. Of course, Kohler had been instrumental in the 1935 reorganization of the American Association of University Instructors in Accounting (AAUIA) into the American Accounting Association. He had encouraged the AAA to begin by expanding its emphasis on research and on the development of accounting theory. It was during his tenure as president of that organization that the "Tentative Statement of Accounting Principles Affecting Corporate Reports" was developed. The Tentative Statement, discussed in greater detail in Chapter 2, was intended to provide a clear, consistent body of principles which would contribute to greater uniformity in financial statement presentation. It was hoped that the propositions articulated in the four-and-one-half-page document would minimize the opportunity to present financial data based on "what will be expedient, plausible or persuasive to investors at any given point in time."[37] It was intended not merely to reflect current practice but to provide a basis for improving it. For example, as discussed in chapter two, neither the all-inclusive concept of income nor the proposed direct write-off of unamortized bond discount at the time of refunding were generally accepted. In fact, conflicts with current practice were recognized as inevitable, since current practice itself already embodied numerous conflicts. The idea was to construct some basic propositions which rest on the primary principle that accounting is a process not of valuation but of cost allocation. The statement was an attempt to establish conceptually sound positions from which the accounting profession could begin to develop a more unified theory of accounting along the lines Kohler had been advocating. In later writings Kohler referred often to the

Tentative Statement, the events surrounding its publication and the propositions it outlined. These references indicate his support for the direction which the AAA adopted in the development of professional standards.

EDUCATION

Kohler believed that progress in the areas of professional standards and research would contribute to progress in accounting education. When accounting practice became better defined, basic decisions about the role of accounting education could be addressed. In the pages of the Accounting Review, Kohler commented on needed developments in the preparation of accountants to accept their professional roles. He was especially concerned with the relative roles of academicians and practitioners, with the use of the CPA examination in a classroom setting and with the education of accountants in schools of business.

Educators and Practitioners

Kohler was convinced that academicians play an important role in the definition of accounting practice. This position became evident in chapter four. That chapter contains a discussion of Kohler's belief that the American Accounting Association was the appropriate body to lead the profession in the development of accounting principles. He feared that the American Institute of Accountants could not see the larger picture clearly enough to contribute significantly to the effort. However, he did not wish to leave the responsibility solely to educators. He emphasized the need for a recognized interdependence of the study and practice of accounting.

Accounting educators, Kohler believed, should keep before them, as if "on the dissecting table,"[38] current practice. Because accounting educators are in a better position than practitioners to maintain a larger perspective, on them falls the primary responsibility for the development of principles which will guide practitioners. By subjecting accounting practice to constant examination and comparison to good theory, they can help to narrow the gap between theory and practice.[39] Moreover, Kohler believed that there need be no such gap. He said that the judgments and everyday experiences of the practitioner could be described in terms of the classroom since the conscientious practitioner follows good theory.[40] By interweaving theory and practice, accounting education can go beyond a "well-ordered collection of procedures" and can broaden the concept and usefulness of the accountant's role.[41]

Education and the CPA Examination

One way in which accounting educators had attempted to close the gap and to prepare students for their roles as practitioners had been their adoption of CPA examination material for classroom use. A problem-oriented approach to teaching leads logically to the inclusion of CPA examination problems in classroom instruction. In addition, because public demands on the profession are constantly changing, instructors depend on CPA examinations as an aid in keeping their teaching material current.[42]

However, Kohler questioned whether the examinations were designed in such a way as to make them appropriate teaching material. He found many of the examination problems too laden with ambiguities to be truly useful for classroom presentation. Problems were vaguely worded; facts were omitted; qualifications and assumptions were necessary. Because such assumptions have no parallel in the real world, where the accountant has access to other records and data and to conversations with the client regarding obscure points, he believed the need for qualifications and assumptions also had no place in examination problems.[43] Although he understood the difficulty of creating examination material free from such ambiguities, he advocated a more thorough advance screening of the questions.

Professional Schools of Accountancy

Kohler questioned whether an accounting program housed within a school of business could provide a sufficiently broad background for the aspiring accountant.[44] A profession, he said, must be recognized by colleges and universities in specialized programs leading to distinct degrees. He found it unfortunate that accountancy was treated by the schools merely as a branch of business. The degrees were limited to such appellations as "bachelor of science in commerce" or "bachelor of business administration" at the undergraduate level, and graduate degrees were similarly labeled as branches of business. Nowhere had accountancy been given the dignity of a separate professional school as had the professions of medicine and law.

Kohler believed the study of accountancy must be separated from schools of business and treated as a distinct social science. Preparation for accounting careers must include general studies in social history, organization, and control, in addition to business and technical studies. Business courses for accounting students should include technological problems in the conduct of specific enterprises. They should exclude some of the managerial courses.[45]

In Kohler's view, the inclusion in the accounting curriculum of both the necessary technical material and studies to enlarge the student's social horizons results in study so specialized as to require a separate school of accountancy. The recognition of accountancy as a profession requiring a separate school must be preceded by a greater research effort on the part of professionals and by a better definition of professional standards. Kohler provided one example:

> An examination of the possible methods of auditing
> would be wasted if the professional objectives of
> audits remained obscure. Likewise, the setting of
> high standards in the conduct of audits would be
> futile if these standards could not be enunciated
> clearly enough for the accounting instructor to
> follow.[46]

He concluded that a better enunciation of standards must precede any meaningful discussion of the role of the accounting educator.

SUMMARY

It has been said that Eric Kohler served as the conscience of the accounting profession. It is certainly true that he monitored professional developments and was outspoken in his criticism of many of them. One of his primary complaints was that many accountants failed to recognize their broader social responsibilities. Such a recognition, he believed, would result in more informative presentation of financial information. It would also curb the tendency of professionals to take measures designed to limit their liability. It would give the accountant an expanded role which would include a full range of advisory services to management, investors, creditors, and the public in general.

A recognition of these responsibilities must be accompanied by a better defined body of accounting standards supported by a thoroughgoing research program which must include a complete consideration of fundamental objectives, opposing ideas, and related literature. This sort of research effort could help to minimize the "agonized copy" which Kohler saw professional bodies grinding out.

Progress in the areas of professional standards and research would then provide the basis for progress in accounting education. Kohler complained that the accounting instructor had to teach procedures because no foundation for principles existed.[47] A better definition of accounting practice would give guidance to the instructor; and the academician, because he has the larger picture more clearly in mind, could then contribute to the development of principles which would better define practice. Kohler emphasized this interdependence of theory and practice. He also questioned the inclusion of accounting studies as a branch of the business curriculum, believing that a profession such as accountancy is best taught in separate professional schools.

NOTES

[1] As related by William W. Cooper, in an interview, it was Roy Kester who referred to Kohler as the profession's conscience.

[2] An open letter to the new editor of the Illinois Certified Public Accountant, handwritten, undated.

[3] Eric L. Kohler, "A Nervous Profession," Accounting Review (December, 1934), p. 334.

[4] Eric L. Kohler, "Audit Extensions," Accounting Review (September, 1939), p. 320.

[5] Eric L. Kohler, "Protection for Auditors," Accounting Review (June, 1931), p. 146.

[6] Eric L. Kohler, "Certificate Revised," Accounting Review (December, 1939), p. 452.

[7] Eric L. Kohler, "The Investor and Financial Statements," Accounting Review (September, 1932), p. 214.

[8] Ultramares Corp. v. Touche (Court of Appeals of New York, 1931, 255 N.Y. 170, 174 N.E. 441) Based upon financial statements audited by Touche, Ross & Co., Ultramares Corporation made loans to Fred Stern & Co. When Stern subsequently went bankrupt, Ultramares showed that Touche had failed to investigate certain fictitious accounts receivable. The decision of the court was that, in order to prove deceit, Ultramares must show false representation, scienter, intent to induce action, reliance on the statements, and resulting damage. The court held that the auditor was not liable to unidentified third parties for negligence short of gross negligence amounting to constructive fraud.

[9] Eric L. Kohler, "The Ultramares Case," Accounting Review (June, 1931), p. 144.

[10] Eric L. Kohler, "Meaningless Certification," Accounting Review (June, 1931), p. 145.

[11] Eric L. Kohler, "Social Significance of Accounting," Accounting Review (September, 1931), p. 230; and "Research Problems," Accounting Review (March, 1931), pp. 80-81.

[12] Eric L. Kohler, "Facts and Purposes," Accounting Review (June, 1933), p. 164.

[13] Ibid.

[14] Eric L. Kohler, "In All My Years," The Accounting Historian (Spring, 1975), p. 4.

[15] Eric L. Kohler, "Standards: A Dialogue," Accounting Review (December, 1935), p. 371.

[16] Eric L. Kohler, "Report of the Committee on Technical Affairs," The Certified Public Accountant (September, 1929), p. 284.

[17] Ibid.

[18] Eric L. Kohler, "Needed: A Research Plan for Accountancy," Accounting Review (March, 1932), pp. 1-10; and "On Developing International Accounting Meanings," International Journal of Accounting, Education and Research (Fall, 1965), pp. 35-40.

[19] Eric L. Kohler, "Corporate Accounts and Reports," Accounting Review (June, 1933), p. 165.

[20] Letter from Eric Kohler to W. W. Cooper, 8 February 1973.

[21] Ibid.

[22] Letter from Eric Kohler to Walter Frese, 3 May 1963.

[23] Letter from Eric Kohler to Richard C. Lytle, 12 December 1967.

[24] Ibid.

[25] Letter to Frese.

[26] Ibid.

[27] Letter from Eric Kohler to Richard C. Lytle, 11 January 1969.

[28]Ibid.

[29]Eric L. Kohler, "And Now the Present," Accounting Review (September, 1939), p. 319.

[30]Eric L. Kohler, "Depreciation and the Price Level, Third Negative," Accounting Review (April, 1948), p. 135.

[31]Eric L. Kohler, "Quasi Reorganizations," Accounting Review (December, 1939), p. 456.

[32]Eric L. Kohler, "The AIA Bulletins on Auditing Procedure," Central States Accounting Conference, 1941, p. 129.

[33]Eric L. Kohler, "Convention Report: Business Meeting of the Association," Report of the President, Accounting Review (March, 1937), p. 71.

[34]Letter from Eric Kohler to J. S. Seidman, 2 March 1965.

[35]Letter from Eric Kohler to Charles E. Noyes, 11 July 1963.

[36]Eric L. Kohler, "Why Not Retain Historical Cost?" Journal of Accountancy (October, 1963), p. 40.

[37]"A Tentative Statement of Accounting Principles Affecting Corporate Reports," Accounting Review (June, 1936), p. 188.

[38]Kohler, "Convention Report," p. 71.

[39]Ibid.

[40]Eric L. Kohler, "Some Principles for Terminologists," Accounting Review (March, 1935), p. 33.

[41]Kohler, "Convention Report," p. 71.

[42]Eric L. Kohler, "Examinations of the American Institute of Accountants," Accounting Review (December, 1927), p. 355.

[43]Ibid., p. 360.

[44]Kohler, "Needed: A Research Plan for Accountancy," p. 4.

[45]<u>Ibid.</u>, p. 5.

[46]<u>Ibid.</u>, p. 7.

[47]Eric L. Kohler, "The Goal of Accounting Education," <u>Experiences with Extensions of Auditing Procedure</u> (American Institute of Accountants, 1940-41), p. 87.

VIII
SUMMARY AND CONCLUSIONS

Although those who knew Eric Kohler best do not claim to have known him well, one cannot examine his writings without becoming aware of certain aspects of his personality, the values he considered paramount, and the tenacity with which he held his beliefs. What emerges repeatedly are, first, an emphasis on simplicity, clarity, and comparability in the compilation and presentation of financial information and, second and more important, an insistence on forthrightness, high principles, and a search for truth. This chapter contains a review and synthesis of the material presented in the preceding chapters in the light of the overriding concerns listed above.

SIMPLICITY, CLARITY, AND COMPARABILITY

In the development of professional standards, in accounting terminology, and in accounting systems developed within governmental agencies, Kohler's goal was finding the simplest means of presenting information in a manner that would facilitate communication and understanding.

Accounting Standards

Principles development

In the development of standards, he stressed the need for a set of fundamental principles which would serve as guidelines in the preparation of financial statements. These principles would, he hoped, provide for some greater degree of uniformity and would thereby promote greater clarity and comparability in the presentation of financial information. As a leader in the reorganization of the American Association of University Instructors in Accounting (AAUIA) and as president of the newly formed American Accounting Association (AAA), Kohler charged a five-man Executive Committee with the task of drafting a statement of such guidelines. The goal was a clear, consistent body of standards which would be intelligible to the layman who is acquainted with business affairs and which, while not demanding rigid uniformity, would constitute an explanation of financial statement content.[1] Many accountants disagreed with the idea of developing such a statement, fearing that they would become cloaked in a straitjacket of rules which would leave little room for the exercise of judgment. Kohler, on the other hand, believed that such a statement was necessary to promote comparability, enhance understanding, and minimize the use of questionable procedures which permit manipulation (for example, charges to surplus and the creation of reserves to smooth income). A clear statement of fundamental principles would, he believed, increase the user's understanding of financial statement information.

The transaction

Recognition of the transaction as the basic building block of accounting provides the basis for developing clear, consistent treatment of financial statement information. According to Kohler, departures from transaction-based treatment only create confusion. One prominent example is the use of current values or index numbers. These highly subjective numbers create a "hodgepodge of valuations" which can only confuse management, stockholders, and analysts.[2]

Income measurement

Another procedure which inhibits communication and comparability is the current operating performance approach to income measurement. The overall objective in the measurement of income is to provide a "common yardstick" which reflects not only revenue and expenses of the current operating period but also those gains and losses recognized in but not strictly applicable to the current period.[3] In Kohler's view the income statement should provide a historical summary reflecting all expenses and losses. The all-inclusive approach to income measurement, like cost-based valuation, provides a more defensible basis for presenting accounting information. Kohler could, then, be expected to endorse the direction in which the profession has moved in income statement presentation.

Accounting Language

Definitions

In the area of accounting terminology, Kohler emphasized his preference for plain, direct language which clearly defines and distinguishes those words which form the accountant's language so that confusion will be minimized. He believed that, where two terms have the same meaning, preference should be given to one of the words; and, where a term has more than one meaning, the separate meanings must be clearly distinguished. Again, clarity and, as a result, more precise communication were the goals.

Vague terms

He attacked those words and phrases which he considered likely to hinder precise communication. Specifically, he cited a list of equivocal adjectives, including adequate, sound, permissible, acceptable, and significant, as attempts to avoid making a simple, readily understandable statement. These terms, he was convinced, were frequently used when members of a committee could not agree or when a committee or an individual wished to avoid taking a position. He cited the excessive use of such terms in official publications as a failure on the part of the profession to accept its responsibility for clear communication with the public.

The audit report

Another notable failure in the area of simple, straightforward communication was the auditor's report. Kohler considered the wording of the report an effort to limit liability through vague or ambiguous phraseology. The language of the report was not, he believed, intended to be understood by the financial statement user. He considered phrases like "We hereby certify, in our opinion" to be designed to minimize communication, to, as he put it, "keep the world adequately mystified."[4]

The profession's attempts at revising the report were likewise unacceptable. Kohler was especially critical of a suggestion that the report begin, "We hereby certify to you." He called the revision an unwelcome effort to limit the auditor's liability to third persons. His position was clear: if the accountant thus wished to limit his liability, he should call himself a private rather than a public accountant.[5] The accountant's responsibility to society at large must be acknowledged, and a simple, direct approach is best: why not simply say "approved" or "approved, with the following qualifications" followed by the name of the accounting firm. The reader then readily understands that the auditor has satisfied himself that the financial position and results of operations of the entity are fairly presented, and such a seal of approval is, after all, what the reader is seeking.

Governmental Accounting

The Tennessee Valley Authority

The same kind of emphasis on simplicity and clarity was the basis for Kohler's reorganization of the accounting processes at the Tennessee Valley Authority (TVA). There he divided and subdivided each area into its smallest possible unit, the activity. Programs and projects were separated into subprograms and subprojects. Each of these subunits was then divided into organizational units. Each organizational unit was the smallest possible administrative subdivision. Each unit was charged with one or more of the activities, but no activity was permitted to extend beyond an organizational unit. Each activity was then clearly and simply described in the organization's accounting manual. Finally, Kohler insisted on clearly defined lines of responsibility so that only one individual was answerable for each activity.

Transactions were recorded by activity, and periodic reports of the month's transactions were submitted to the activity head by the fifth of the following month. Reports were kept as simple as possible, and they were to be designed for the recipient. Kohler was determined to put out no more in the way of reports than would actually be used. He encouraged agency controllers to discover the needs of each individual activity head and to design reports to meet those needs.

A further simplification inherent in the TVA system was the avoidance, insofar as possible, of allocations and prorations of cost. Activity heads were held responsible only for those costs which could be traced to them by a simple, one-step process. Costs were then summarized upward rather than allocated and prorated downward. When allocations were necessary, as they were for TVA's massive joint and common costs related to dams, purchased land rights, removal of trees and houses from prospective reservoirs, construction of access roads to lakes behind the dams, and so forth, Kohler recognized the arbitrary nature of the proposed methods for such allocations; and he recommended accepting none of the proposals and, instead, allocating those costs to power, navigation, and flood control on a judgment basis.

Other governmental agencies

Kohler simplified the accounting processes at the Tennessee Valley Authority by installing good accounting controls adapted from commercial accounting. And he recommended the simplification of governmental accounting in general by making public sector accounting practices conform more closely to those of the private sector. He believed the interests of simplicity and clarity would best be served by teaching governmental officials the language of businessmen.

One simplification is removing the practice of booking budgets and encumbrances, substituting instead a memorandum budget ledger which provides the necessary information in the simplest possible form. The accounts are then uncomplicated by committed but unexpended amounts. In addition to the revised treatment of budgetary items, a well-defined classification of accounts also contributes to clarity and comparability. Finally, an activity accounting system, fortified by prompt, easily understood reports and overseen by a controller, contributes essentially to solving what Kohler viewed as the deficiencies in governmental accounting.

Summary

Simple, clear, unequivocal presentation of financial information, then, requires a threefold effort. First, careful definition of the accountant's language provides the foundation. Second, this precise terminology must be the basis for the formulation of accounting standards which promote greater uniformity and provide guidance for financial reporting. Third, the sort of communication which precise definition and carefully formulated standards provide for external users must also be provided internally for decision making. Elements of the accounting system must be defined and the system itself constructed so that lines of authority, responsibility, and communication are clear and direct.

TRUTH AND HIGH PRINCIPLES

Underlying Kohler's insistence on clarity in the definition of terms and standards was an insistence on eliminating both ambiguity and the possibility of manipulation. His commitment to truth and high principles permeated his efforts in the development of accounting standards, accounting language, accounting systems, and professional practices.

Accounting Standards

His high principles were evident in his approach to standards development. His advocacy of greater uniformity and full disclosure were a part of his desire to see that information is complete, that nothing is concealed. The insistence on historical cost came not only from a belief that cost-based information was more useful to decision makers but also from a conviction that value-based information would be too subjective and would open the door to various manipulative practices. Also essential to forthright, objective presentation of financial information is the adoption of the all-inclusive income statement. A series of income statements of an enterprise must provide a historical summary of all revenues, expenses, gains, and losses of the business. To allow charges to surplus accounts or the creation of reserves distorts the picture and impedes financial statement disclosure. Again, the door to manipulative practices would be opened. Careful definition of earned surplus and a clear distinction between paid-in capital and earned surplus also promote a straightforward approach to the presentation of financial information about the entity. Just as Kohler disapproved of charges to retained earnings, he, in general, expressed concern about other expedient but theoretically questionable positions. This attitude characterized his objection to the current operating performance approach to income measurement, the application to inventories of a last-in-first-out cost flow assumption, the provision for accelerated depreciation, and other tax-saving schemes.

Of course, Kohler was impatient with compromise, and he believed that many of the compromises which had been made were unnecessary. He did not hesitate to speak out when he believed questionable treatments had been adopted. The treatments of deferred taxes and of the investment tax credit (as outlined in Accounting Principles Board Opinion No. 2) provide examples. The measurement of income on other than an all-inclusive basis is a prime example.

Accounting Language

The same sort of concern may be found in his objection to the use of those adjectives which he termed vague and equivocal. They are employed to avoid an open, truthful approach to a problem. Thus, their use may enable a committee to reach agreement by permitting the same words to say different things to different people. The degree of uniformity and informative disclosure which Kohler considered essential was compromised when such terms were employed. Again, the auditor's report provided an example of an attempt to avoid candid communication. The auditor who would adopt high principles and search for truthful, complete communication would have no need to construct his report so as to minimize his liability.

Governmental Accounting

Kohler's writings and practices in the governmental area provide several examples of his dedication to high principles. One such example is found in his insistence on the importance of an organization's internal auditor as the conscience and moral watchdog of the organization. An even better one is provided by his attitude toward his position as controller of the Marshall Plan: one of his colleagues has referred to what he calls "the Kohler way," by which he means a way which emphasizes high principles. He has recalled that the way that he was able to get Kohler's concurrence on a number of matters was to identify his proposals with high moral precepts, thus applying Kohler's own guidelines, which were weighted heavily by such considerations.[6] And, of course, the incident related by W. W. Cooper and Yuji Ijiri (page 28) regarding Kohler's willingness to resign rather than compromise epitomizes his insistence on a code of conduct which emphasizes this approach and the lengths to which he was willing to go for the sake of his principles.

The Profession

Some of Kohler's strongest statements regarding the high principles which accountants should embrace were made in the pages of the Accounting Review during his years as editor of the periodical. He criticized what he saw as the smug self-satisfaction of professionals who were content to allow their national organization to function primarily as a gentlemen's club. He was convinced that any group who considered its basic purpose to be providing the opportunity for its members to get together to behave as gentlemen toward one another was unaware of the things that were truly at stake in the profession.

He urged professionals to accept the broad social responsibilities which the term public accountant implied. He believed that accountants had profound obligations to third parties and that they must recognize their duties as extending beyond those related to an entity's management.

Kohler believed that the auditor stands in a unique position to protect the public from unscrupulous business practices and is negligent if he ignores his obligation to the world and sees his duty strictly in terms of a responsibility to the management of the organization.

Kohler encouraged accountants to work to raise the level of honesty and fair practice in business. He believed that the accountant can contribute to intelligent competition and social welfare by measuring costs and providing reports which can be related to wages, prices, and budgeting. The accountant is ideally a business advisor in the formation, combination, and dissolution of corporations; he is one who can promote good financial practice, including full, forthright disclosure; he stands as agent between stockholder and corporation, capital and labor, debtor and creditor. In this expanded role he must have the good of society as his objective.

According to Kohler, a necessary prerequisite to the accountant's broader role is the establishment of a thoroughgoing research program aimed at narrowing the gap between theory and practice. The expedients which practitioners are called upon to adopt may compromise theoretically sound positions. Accountants must work to make these necessary compromises fewer in number. Those accountants who make up the academic arm of the profession are in an ideal position to contribute importantly to this goal since they have before them the larger picture.

Summary

Kohler's commitment to truth and high principles was evident in his professional life and in his professional writings. Greater uniformity and full disclosure, he believed, would provide more complete, more objective information. Careful definition and the use of precise terminology would contribute to informative disclosure. By the same token, high moral principles must weigh importantly in the construction and monitoring of accounting systems for public or private sector organizations. Finally, he believed that it is the accountant's responsibility to protect the public and to promote honest and fair practice in business.

CONCLUSION

"The accountant is bound to tell the truth," Kohler said. "If the truth hurts, should it be glossed over?"[7] His answer to this question is clearly "no." His insistence on the development of principles, his search for precise terminology, and his approach to public service testify to his own high principles. His biting criticism of professional compromises testifies to the fact that he expected the profession as a whole to embrace those same high principles. He believed that such an approach was inherent in the very title "certified public accountant." He found satisfaction with the state of accountancy at any point in time unacceptable. He was impatient with attempts to limit the accountant's role. He expected professionals to be continuously searching for a means of producing and providing better, more complete, more truthful information. The accountant is not only bound to tell the truth; he is also bound to a continuous search for it.

NOTES

[1] "A Statement of Objectives of the American Accounting Association," Accounting Review (March, 1936), p. 1.

[2] Eric L. Kohler, "Why Not Retain Historical Cost," Journal of Accountancy (October, 1963), p. 40.

[3] Eric L. Kohler, "Some Tentative Propositions Underlying Consolidated Reports," Accounting Review (March, 1938), p. 67.

[4] Eric L. Kohler, "Modernizing Certificates," Accounting Review (September, 1931), p. 231.

[5] Eric L. Kohler, "Protection for Auditors," Accounting Review (June, 1931), p. 146.

[6] Samuel Nakasian, "Eric Kohler in the Marshall Plan," in Eric Louis Kohler: Accounting's Man of Principles, W. W. Cooper and Yuji Ijiri, editors (Reston, Virginia: Reston Publishing Company, 1979), p. 101.

[7] Eric L. Kohler, "Tendencies in Balance Sheet Construction," Accounting Review (December, 1926), p. 7.

BIBLIOGRAPHY

Published Works of Eric Louis Kohler:

Kohler, Eric L. "Accountant Suggests Improvements in Income Tax Law." The American Accountant, August, 1927, pp. 13-17.

_____. "Accountants' Reports and Certificates." The Robert Morris Associates Monthly Bulletin, July, 1929, pp. 50-56.

_____. "Accounting as a Management Control." Municipal Finance, August, 1948, pp. 3-8.

_____. "Accounting Concepts and National Income." Accounting Review, January, 1952, pp. 50-56.

_____. The Accounting Exchange: "A C.P.A. Problem." Accounting Review, December, 1931, pp. 308-311.

"A Federal Income-Tax Chart for 1936." Accounting Review, December, 1935, pp. 406-407.

"Grading C.P.A. Papers." Accounting Review, June, 1932, pp. 142-144.

"Solution to Problem in December Issue." Accounting Review, March, 1932, pp. 67-69.

"Two C.P.A. Problems." Accounting Review, December, 1932, pp. 296-330.

_____. Accounting for Business Executives. Chicago, Illinois: A. W. Shaw, 1927.

_____. _Accounting for Management._ Englewood Cliffs, New Jersey: Prentice-Hall, Inc., 1965.

_____. "Accounting for the TVA." _Accounting Forum_, June 1941, pp. 48-51.

_____, and Howard W. Wright. _Accounting in the Federal Government._ Englewood Cliffs, New Jersey: Prentice-Hall, Inc., 1956.

_____. "Accounting Practices in State Agencies." _Journal of Accountancy_, August, 1959, pp. 52-60.

_____. _Accounting Principles Underlying Federal Income Taxes._ Chicago, Illinois: A. W. Shaw, 1924 and 1925.

_____. "Accounting Progress in the Federal Government." _Illinois Society of C.P.A.'s Bulletin_, September, 1945, pp. 10-13.

_____. "Accounting Principles Underlying Corporate Financial Statements." _Accounting Review_, June, 1941.

_____. "Accounting Problems of a Governmental Agency." _Federal Government Accounting._

_____. "Accounting Theory as Affected by Federal Income Taxation." _Papers and Proceedings of the American Association of University Instructors in Accounting_, December, 1922, pp. 73-83.

_____. "The Activity: Nerve Center of Management and Accounting." _N.A.C.A. Bulletin_, August, 1955, pp. 1627-1633.

_____. "Administrative Development of Financial Controls in Government." _Municipal Finance_, May 1941, pp. 4-10.

_____ "The AIA Bulletins on Auditing Procedure." Central States Accounting Conference, 1941, pp. 123-129.

_____. Advanced Accounting Problems. Englewood Cliffs, New Jersey: Prentice-Hall, Inc., 1939 and 1947.

_____. "Amendment of Regulation S-X." The Illinois Certified Public Accountant, March, 1951, pp. 50-55.

_____. "Aspects of National Income: Foreword." Accounting Review, April, 1953, p. 178.

_____. "Background for Management Accounting Techniques." N.A.A. Bulletin, October, 1961, pp. 5-16.

_____. "Balance Sheet Standards." The Certified Public Accountant, December, 1931, pp. 373-376.

_____. "Basic Concepts in the Reorganization of State Accounting and Auditing Practices." The Illinois Certified Public Accountant, Winter, 1956-57, pp. 7-9.

_____. "Changing Concepts of Business Income." The Ohio Certified Public Accountant, Summer, 1952, pp. 1-7.

_____. "Comments on TVA Audit." Journal of Accountancy, April, 1948, pp. 337-338.

_____. "The Concept of Earned Surplus." Accounting Review, September, 1931, pp. 206-217.

_____. "Convention Report: Business Meeting of the Association." Accounting Review, March, 1937, p. 71.

_____. "Costs, Prices and Profits: Accounting in the War Program." Accounting Review, July, 1945, pp. 267-308.

_____. "Depreciation and the Price Level, A Symposium: Third Negative." Accounting Review, April, 1948, pp. 131-136.

_____. "The Development of Accounting for Regulatory Purposes by the Federal Power Commission." Accounting Review, January, 1946, pp. 19-31.

_____. A Dictionary for Accountants. Englewood Cliffs, New Jersey: Prentice-Hall, Inc., 1952, 1957, 1963, 1970, and 1975.

_____. "Essential Elements in a Program of Internal Audit." The Federal Accountant, January, 1952, pp. 9-15.

_____. "Examinations of the American Institute of Accountants." Accounting Review, December, 1927, pp. 354-361.

_____. "Expenditure Controls in the United States Government." Accounting Review, January, 1945, pp. 31-44.

_____. "Fairness." Journal of Accountancy, December, 1967, pp. 58-60.

_____. Federal Income Taxes. Chicago: A. W. Shaw, 1967.

_____. "Financing European Recovery." Papers of the 23rd Annual Michigan Accounting Conference, 23 October 1948, pp. 14-18.

_____. "The First Course In Accounting." ExLibris, February, 1927, pp. 5-7.

_____. "The Goal of Accounting Education." Experiences with Extensions of Auditing Procedure, American Institute of Accountants, 1940-41, pp. 84-88.

_____. "How Much Depreciation." Illinois Society of C.P.A.'s Bulletin, December, 1947, pp. 4-9.

_____. "Inadmissible Assets and Invested Capital." Papers and Proceedings of the American Association of University Instructors in Accounting, December, 1919, pp. 37-41.

_____. "In All My Years." The Accounting Historian, Spring, 1975, pp. 4,6.

_____. "Investment Stock Costs Under the 1921 Revenue Act." University of Minnesota Administration, January, 1923, pp. 86-94.

_____. "The Jenkins Report." Accounting Review, April, 1963, pp. 266-269.

_____. "Management Improvement in the Department of Defense." The Federal Accountant, Fall, 1966, pp. 122-128.

_____. "Needed: A Research Plan for Accountancy." Accounting Review, March, 1932, pp. 1-10.

_____. "New Accounting Conceptions in the Revenue Act of 1924." The National Income Tax Magazine, January, 1925, pp. 17-21.

_____. "Notes on Activity Accounting." International Journal of Accounting, Education and Research, Spring, 1967, pp. 58-60.

_____. "On Developing International Accounting Meaning." International Journal of Accounting, Education and Research, Fall, 1965, pp. 35-40.

_____. "Policy and Administration in Board-Executive Relationships." Business and Society, Autumn, 1965, pp. 20-24.

_____. Practice Problems in Auditing. New York: Prentice-Hall, 1955.

_____. "Price Policies and Procurement Practices in the ECA Program." Address before the National Association of Purchasing Agents Convention, Chicago. The Chicago Purchasor, August, 1949, pp. 42-45.

_____, and Paul L. Morrison. Principles of Accounting. Chicago, Illinois: A. W. Shaw, 1926.

_____. Principles of Accounting. New York: McGraw Hill, 1931.

_____, and Paul W. Pettengill. Principles of Auditing. Chicago, Illinois: A. W. Shaw, 1924 and 1927.

_____, and Paul W. Pettengill. Principles of Auditing. New York: McGraw Hill, 1932.

_____. "Problems of Accounting Research: Some Principles for Terminologists." Accounting Review, March, 1935, pp. 31-33.

_____. "Purview of the Government Accountant." The Federal Accountant, Spring, 1966, pp. 6-19.

_____. "Recent Developments in the Formulation of Accounting Principles." Accounting Research, January, 1953, pp. 30-55.

_____. "Reorganizations and the Federal Income Tax Law." The National Income Tax Magazine, May, 1926, pp. 161-163, 178-180.

_____. "Report of the Committee on Technical Affairs." The Certified Public Accountant, September, 1929, pp. 283-384.

_____. "Research Potentials in International Accounting." Proceedings of the International Conference on Accounting Education, 1952, pp. 87-92.

_____. "Restoration of Fixed Asset Values to the Balance Sheet: First Negative." Accounting Review, April, 1947, pp. 200-203.

_____. "Some Debated Issues on Consolidated Financial Statements." Papers on Accounting Principles and Procedures, 1938, pp. 42-46.

_____. "Some Principles for Terminologists." Accounting Review, March, 1935, pp. 31-33.

_____. "Some Tentative Propositions Underlying Consolidated Reports." Accounting Review, March, 1938, pp. 63-73.

_____. "Something About Accounting Language." Massachusetts Society of C.P.A.'s News Bulletin, October, 1954, pp. 2-5.

_____. "Something About Definitions." The Illinois Certified Public Accountant, September, 1951, pp. 1-9.

_____. "Standards: A Dialogue." Accounting Review, December, 1935, pp. 370-379.

_____. "A Statement of Objectives of the American Accounting Association." Accounting Review, March, 1936, p. 1.

_____. "Surplus." Contemporary Accounting. American Institute of Accountants, 1945, pp. 1-15.

_____. "The TVA and Its Power-Accounting Problems." Accounting Review, January, 1948, pp. 44-62.

_____. Tennessee Valley Authority Oral History. Memphis, Tennessee: Memphis State University Oral History Research Office, February, 1971.

_____. Theories and Practice:

"And Now the Present." Accounting Review, September, 1939, pp. 318-319.

"Audit Extensions." Accounting Review, September, 1939, pp. 319-321.

"Bond Discount." Accounting Review, December, 1939, pp. 454-456.

"Cases in Accounting." Accounting Review, March, 1940, pp. 130-131.

"Certificate Revised." Accounting Review, December, 1939, pp. 452-453.

"Deficiencies in Federal Accounting." Accounting Review, September, 1940, pp. 443-446.

"Federal Accounting: Institute Research." Accounting Review, March, 1940, pp. 128-130.

"Looking Backward." Accounting Review, September, 1939, pp. 316-318.

"Need for Budgetary Accounts." Accounting Review, December, 1940, pp. 528-530.

"Protection for Investors." Accounting Review, September, 1940, pp. 446-452.

Theories and Practice, continued:

"Some Old 'Rules' Revived." Accounting Review, December, 1939, pp. 453-454.

"Quasi Reorganizations." Accounting Review, December, 1939, p. 456.

"What of the Future?" Accounting Review, September, 1939, p. 321.

_____. "What is Ahead for the Accounting Profession?" Proceedings of the Fifth Annual Institute on Accounting, May, 1942, pp. 20-34.

_____. "Why Not Retain Historical Cost?" Journal of Accountancy, October, 1963, pp. 35-41.

Unpublished Works of Eric Kohler:

From the personal files of Eric L. Kohler. Department of Accounting and Information Systems, J. L. Kellogg Graduate School of Management, Northwestern University, Evanston, Illinois.

Kohler, Eric L. "Accountants and Cost." Typewritten article. Undated.

_____. "Accountant's Responsibility." Typewritten address presented at Ann Arbor Alumni Conference, 19 May 1939.

_____. "Accounting for Municipally Owned Assets." Typewritten address presented before the Municipal Finance Officers Association. Undated.

_____. "Activity Accounting--A Concept of Cost Control." Typewritten address. Undated.

_____. "The 'Activity' as a Basis for Fiscal Controls in the TVA." Typewritten address presented before the Society for the Advancement of Management, 17 November 1943.

_____. "Can Accounting, As It Is Taught, And Accounting, As It Is Practiced, Bear a Greater Family Resemblance?" Typewritten notes. Undated.

_____. "Chicago's Road to Democracy." Typewritten panel discussion with Henry P. Chandler and Ernest O. Melby, Lecture Number Seven, Lecture Reporting Service, Chicago, 6 December 1936.

_____. "Comments on the Exposure Draft 'Reporting the Results of Operations.'" Typewritten paper, 1 November 1936.

——————. "Discussion of Accounting Principles and Standards Prescribed for Federal Agencies by the Comptroller
General of the United States." Typewritten summary of
speech presented at the Brookings Institution Accountants
Forum. Undated.

——————. "From One Editor to Another." Handwritten open
letter to the new editor of the Illinois Certified Public
Accountant. Undated.

——————. "Local Government Audits." Typewritten article.
Undated.

——————. "Meeting of the A.A.U.I.A. in New York." Typewritten memorandum prepared by Kohler for Arthur
Andersen, reporting on the December 27–28, 1935, meeting,
2 January 1936.

——————. "Memo to Members of the Committee on Technical
Affairs. Typewritten memorandum. Undated.

——————. "Memorandum on Letter from Paul Grady Dated
November 27, 1934." Typewritten memorandum. Undated.

——————. "Memorandum on Management-Engineering Curriculum
of Carnegie Institute of Technology." Typewritten memorandum to Provost Elliott Dunlap Smith, October, 1952.

——————. "Memorandum on Sales and Cost of Sales." Typewritten. Undated.

——————. "Notes on Fiscal Reorganization in the State of
Illinois." Typewritten notes prepared at the request of
Lloyd Morey, State Auditor, August, 1956.

——————. "Notes on Fiscal Reorganization of the Federal
Fiscal Administration." Typewritten notes, October, 1938.

_____. "An Outsider Looks at the GAO Manual." Typewritten address presented before a joint meeting of the Dayton chapters of the Federal Government Accountants Association and the Institute of Internal Auditors, 26 February 1959.

_____. "Professor Sanders' Paper on Financial Reports to Stockholders." Typewritten review prepared for Arthur Andersen, 20 April 1934.

_____. "The Role of Accounting in the Development of Administrative Techniques." Typewritten address. Undated.

_____. "Social Accounting." Typewritten article. Undated.

_____. "A Statement by E. L. Kohler Before the Military Affairs Committee." Typewritten statement. June, 1941.

_____. "A Statement of Accounting Principles." Typewritten article. Undated.

_____. "Suggestions for a Memorandum to be Issued to State Agencies by the Auditor of Public Accounts." Typewritten comments. Undated.

_____. "Suggestions for Specifications for Internal Auditor." Typewritten comments. 13 December 1956.

_____. "Summary of Minimum Points Which Should Be Included in Annual Reports to Stockholders." Typewritten comments. Undated.

_____. Testimony in Spring, 1947, for Presentation to Senate Public Works Committee in Connection with S. 1277. Typewritten testimony. Spring, 1947.

_____. "What Can Accounting Contribute to Management?" Typewritten panel discussion, meeting of Federal Government Accountants Association, Washington chapter. Undated.

EDITORIALS, Accounting Review:

"Audit Extensions." September, 1939, pp. 319-322.

"Business Versus the Public." June, 1933, pp. 162-163.

"Capital Surplus." September, 1934, pp. 254-256.

"Corporate Accounts and Reports." June, 1933, pp. 164-165.

"The Court on Appreciation." March, 1930, pp. 76-78.

"Dated Surplus." September, 1934, pp. 256-257.

"Earned Surplus." September, 1929, pp. 192-193.

"Earned Surplus." September, 1930, pp. 252-253.

"Economists and Costs." September, 1934, pp. 258-261.

"Ethics for the Tyro." September, 1929, pp. 248-250.

"Facts and Purposes." June, 1933, pp. 163-164.

"The Investor and Financial Statements." September, 1932,
    pp. 214-216.

"Meaningless Certification." June, 1931, pp. 144-145.

"Modernizing Certificates." September, 1931, pp. 231-232.

"A Nervous Profession." December, 1934, p. 334.

"New Definitions." September, 1934, p. 261.

"Overburdened Terms."   June, 1931, pp. 142-143.

"Problems and Cases." September, 1929, pp. 247-248.

"Pro-Forma Balance Sheets."   September, 1933, pp. 243-244.

"Professional Examinations."   March, 1930, pp. 75-76.

"Protection for Auditors."   June, 1931, pp. 145-146.

"Providing a Substitute."   September, 1933, pp. 244-245.

"The Public Utility Holding Company."   December, 1932,
    pp. 301-305.

"Purists."   September, 1930, p. 253.

"Research Problems."   March, 1931, pp. 80-82.

"Scanning."   September, 1934, pp. 257-258.

"Social Significance of Accounting."   September, 1931,
    pp. 230-231.

"Standards Must Come."   December, 1934, pp. 334-336.

"Suggestions for Write-Downs."   March, 1931, pp. 80-82.

"Terminology for Accountants."   September, 1931, p. 232.

"The Ultramares Case."   June, 1931, pp. 143-144.

LETTERS FROM E. L. KOHLER TO:

(From the personal files of Eric L. Kohler. Department of Accounting and Information Systems, J. L. Kellogg Graduate School of Management, Northwestern University, Evanston, Illinois.)

T. Coleman Andrews, 11 September 1946.

Robert Anthony, 22 November 1965.

Robert Anthony and Robert Sprouse, 29 November 1963.

Marshall Armstrong, 5 November 1973.

James J. Bacci, 31 March 1953.

Carman Blough, 29 October 1937.

Carman Blough, 3 February 1958.

F. Sewell Bray, 21 September 1951.

Victor Z. Brink, Undated.

William L. Campfield, 1 November 1926.

John Carey, 22 February 1950.

Richard Castle, 10 May 1965.

Richard Castle, 29 June 1965.

William W. Cooper, 8 February 1973.

Mr. Corson, 30 January 1945.

Shirley Covington, 7 October 1974.

Gifford Cruze, October 1965.

Editor, The Accountant, 5 February 1963.

Editor, Chicago Tribune, 6 February 1940.

Editor, Chicago Tribune, 26 February 1940.

Ronald S. Edwards, 11 October 1937.

G. S. Ellsworth, 18 November 1943.

Walter Frese, 3 May 1963.

President Hutchins, 9 May 1936.

Secretary Ickes, 25 September 1943.

Estes Kefauver, 30 April 1951.

A. C. Littleton, 6 November 1962.

Richard C. Lytle, 29 August 1966.

Richard C. Lytle, 12 December 1967.

Richard C. Lytle, 11 January 1969.

James McCoy, 24 January 1959.

Lloyd Morey, 11 March 1963.

Mary Murphy, 27 January 1956

Raymond Nassimbene, 22 January 1956.

William A. Newman, Jr., 3 February 1958.

J. C. Nixon, 11 December 1975.

Charles E. Noyes, 11 July 1963.

Norris Poulson, 22 February 1950.

John W. Queenan, 16 December 1963.

Donald Schaeffer, 4 December 1974.

DR Scott, 18 August 1937.

J. S. Seidman, 2 March 1965.

Harold D. Smith, 14 August 1944.

Elmer Staats, 9 July 1973.

E. Arnold Sunstrom, 6 January 1950.

E. Arnold Sunstrom, 28 March, 1950.

E. Arnold Sunstrom, 14 September 1951.

Leonard Spacek, 6 January 1950.

Lawrence Vance, 14 May 1957.

Howard Warrington, April 1974.

Frank Weitzel, 10 June 1966.

Garret White, 10 January 1973

Garret White, 15 April 1974.

Stephen A. Zeff, 31 July 1971.

BOOK REVIEWS

The Elusive Art of Accounting by Howard Ross. Journal of Accountancy, August, 1966, pp. 87-89.

Federal Income Taxation by Joseph J. Klein. Accounting Review, September, 1931, pp. 245-246.

The Federal Taxing Process by Roy Blough. Accounting Review, January, 1931, pp. 153-154.

An Interpretation of Accounts by Thomas A. Budd and Edward Needles Wright. Accounting Review, September, 1928, pp. 212-213.

"Language of Accounting." Journal of Accountancy, August, 1957, p. 91.

Professional Accounting in 25 Countries by Committee on International Relations. Accounting Review, October, 1965, p. 922.

ADDITIONAL SOURCES:

American Accounting Association. "Accounting and Reporting
    Standards for Corporate Financial Statements: 1957
    Revision." Accounting Review, October, 1957,
    pp. 536-546.

American Accounting Association. "Accounting Concepts and
    Standards Underlying Corporate Financial Statements:
    1948 Revision." Accounting Review, October, 1948,
    pp. 339-344.

American Accounting Association. "Accounting Principles
    Underlying Corporate Financial Statements." Accounting
    Review, June, 1941, pp. 133-139.

American Accounting Association. A Statement of Basic
    Accounting Theory. Evanston, Illinois: American
    Accounting Association, 1966.

American Accounting Association. A Statement on Accounting
    Theory and Theory Acceptance. Sarasota, Florida:
    American Accounting Association, 1977.

American Accounting Association. "A Tentative Statement of
    Accounting Principles Affecting Corporate Reports."
    Accounting Review, June, 1936, pp. 187-191.

Blough, Carman G. "The Need for Accounting Principles."
    Accounting Review, March, 1937, pp. 30-37.

Brinks, Victor Z. "Further Meanings Underlying Auditing
    Instructions." Journal of Accountancy, February,
    164-165.

Burns, Thomas J., and Edward N. Coffman. The Accounting
    Hall of Fame: Profiles of Thirty-Six Members. College
    of Administrative Science, The Ohio State University,
    1976.

Carey, John L. "The CPA's Professional Heritage." _Accounting Historians Working Papers_, Volumes I and II. Atlanta, Georgia: The Academy of Accounting Historians, 1975.

_____. _The Rise of the Accounting Profession: From Technician to Professional_. New York: American Institute of Certified Public Accountants, 1969.

Chatfield,Michael, editor. _Contemporary Studies in the Evolution of Accounting Thought_. Belmont, California: Dickenson Publishing Company, Inc., 1968.

Coffman, Edward N., editor. _The Academy of Accounting Historians Working Papers_, Volumes I and II. Atlanta: Georgia: Academy of Accounting Historians, 1975.

Cooper, W. W., and Yuji Ijiri, editors. _Eric Louis Kohler: Accounting's Man of Principles_. Reston, Virginia: Reston Publishing Co., 1979.

_____. _Kohler's Dictionary for Accountants_. Englewood Cliffs, New Jersey: Prentice Hall, Inc., 1982.

_____, and Gary John Previts. _Eric Louis Kohler: A Collection of His Writing (1919-1975)_. Atlanta, Georgia: The Academy of Accounting Historians, 1980.

Deinzer, Harvey T. _Development of Accounting Thought_. New York: Holt, Rinehart and Winston, Inc., 1965.

Dixon, Robert L., and Harry D. Kerrigan. "Criticisms of the Tentative Statement of Accounting Principles." _Accounting Review_, March, 1941, pp. 49-65.

Edwards, James Don. _History of Public Accounting in the United States_. East Lansing, Michigan: Michigan State University Business Studies, 1960.

Edwards, James Don, and Roland F. Salmonson. Contributions
    of Four Accounting Pioneers. East Lansing, Michigan:
    Michigan State University Business Studies, 1961.

"Eric Kohler Honored." News Report, Journal of Accountancy,
    July, 1961, pp. 14, 16.

Federal Reserve Board. Uniform Accounting. Washington,
    D. C.: Government Printing Office, 1917.

Fite, Gilbert C., and Jim E. Reese. An Economic History of
    the United States. Boston: Houghton Mifflin Company,
    1959.

Greer, Howard C. "Applications of Accounting Rules and
    Standards to Financial Statements." Accounting Review,
    December, 1938.

_____. "Benchmarks and Beacons." Accounting Review,
    January, 1956.

_____. "What Are Accepted Principles of Accounting."
    Accounting Review, March, 1938, pp. 25-31.

Healy, Robert E. "The Next Step in Accounting." Account-
    ing Review, March, 1938, pp. 1-9.

Husband, George R. "Accounting Postulates: An Analysis of
    the Tentative Statement of Accounting Principles."
    Accounting Review, December, 1937, pp. 386-406.

Littleton, A. C. "The Relation of Function to Principles."
    Accounting Review, September, 1938, pp. 233-241.

_____. "Suggestions for the Revision of the Tentative
    Statement of Accounting Principles." Accounting Review,
    March, 1939, pp. 57-64.

Marias, Julian. <u>Generations: A Historical Method</u>.
    Tuscaloosa, Alabama: University of Alabama
    Press, 1970.

Mautz, R. K. "Revising the Tentative Statement." <u>Account-
    ing Review</u>, March, 1941, pp. 66-75

_____, and Gary John Previts. "Eric Kohler: An
    Accounting Original." <u>Accounting Review</u>, April,
    1977, pp. 301-307.

Nelson, Edward G. "A Note on Principles of Accounting."
    <u>Accounting Review</u>, December, 1939, pp. 350-355.

Nolan, James. "It's Much More Than a Dictionary." <u>Journal
    of Accountancy</u>, May, 1972, pp. 20, 22, 24.

<u>Papers and Proceedings of the Fifth Annual Meeting</u>, Ameri-
    can Association of University Instructors in Accounting.
    March, 1921.

<u>Papers and Proceedings of the Seventh Annual Meeting</u>, Amer-
    ican Association of University Instructors in Accounting.
    April, 1923.

<u>Papers and Proceedings of the Eighth Annual Meeting</u>, Ameri-
    can Association of University Instructors in Accounting.
    June, 1924.

<u>Papers and Proceedings of the Ninth Annual Meeting</u>, Ameri-
    can Association of University Instructors in Accounting.
    February, 1925.

Previts, Gary John, and Barbara Dubis Merino. <u>A History of
    Accounting in America</u>. New York: John Wiley and Sons,
    1979.

Rorem, C. Rufus. "Accounting Theory: A Critique of the
    Tentative Statement of Accounting Principles." <u>Account-
    ing Review</u>, June, 1937, pp. 133-138.

Ross, Howard. "Author Replies to Reviewer of 'The Elusive Art of Accounting.'" Journal of Accountancy, September, 1966, pp. 26, 28, 30, 32-33.

Sanders, T. H. "Comments on the Statement of Accounting Principles." Accounting Review, March, 1937, pp. 76-79.

_____. "The Development of Accounting Principles." Accounting Review, March, 1935, pp. 100-102.

Scott, DR. "The Tentative Statement of Principles." Accounting Review, September, 1937, pp. 296-303.

Scovill, H. T. "Reflections of Twenty-Five Years in the American Accounting Association." Accounting Review, June, 1941, pp. 167-175.

"A Statement of Objectives of the American Accounting Association." Accounting Review, March, 1936, p. 1.

Stempf, Victor H. "A Critique of the Tentative Statement of Accounting Principles." Accounting Review, March, 1938, pp. 55-62.

Storey, Reed K. The Search for Accounting Principles. New York: American Institute of Certified Public Accountants, 1964.

U. S. Congress. Joint Committee on the Investigation of the Tennessee Valley Authority. Hearings, Parts 13 and 14. Washington, D. C.: Government Printing Office, 1939.

U. S. Congress. Senate. Report of the Joint Committee on the Investigation of the Tennessee Valley Authority. S. Doc 56, 76th Cong., 1st sess., 1939.

Zeff, Stephen A., editor. The American Accounting Association: Its First Fifty Years. Evanston, Illinois: American Accounting Association, 1966.

ERIC LOUIS KOHLER

IN THE

ACCOUNTING PROFESSION

by Nancy A. Wagner

With this book, the author presents one of the first in-depth studies of Eric Louis Kohler's contribution to the accounting profession. The book reflects Kohler's emphasis on the development of accounting principles, his concern with uniform terminology and precise communication, and his interest in the contribution of accounting to management. Called "one of the accounting giants of this century," Kohler sought to bring simplicity, clarity, and comparability into the compilation and presentation of financial information.

Georgia State University—Degrees of Excellence   ISBN 0-88406-196-5